D1135425

Play Ten

Ten short plays by James Saunders,
David Selbourne, N.F. Simpson,
Vivienne Welburn and Olwen Wymark

Edited by Robin Rook

Edward Arnold

British Library Cataloguing in Publication Data

Play Ten.
    1.   English drama
    I.   Rook, Robin
    822'.9'1408   PR1272

    ISBN 0-7131-0156-3

This edition first published 1977 by
Edward Arnold (Publishers) Ltd
41 Bedford Square, London WC1B 3DQ

Edward Arnold (Australia) Pty Ltd
80 Waverley Road
Caulfield East
Victoria 3145
Australia

Reprinted 1979, 1980, 1982, 1986

Set IBM by 𝍤 Tek-Art, Croydon, Surrey

Printed in Great Britain by
Spottiswoode Ballantyne Ltd., Colchester and London

Contents

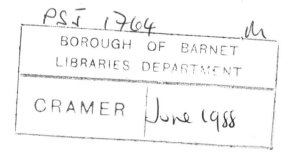

Introduction

It is easy to appreciate a play in performance, difficult to imagine that performance from reading the text. It is in some ways as difficult as reading music. Stage directions only hint at the action on stage and the emotional pointing of lines. They give the barest outline of characterization and setting. Play texts provide the raw material which actors and directors fashion into a living form. When plays cease to do this, they start to encroach on the novel.

Essentially, the playwright has to embody the performance in the dialogue. From the words a character speaks, the reader slowly builds up an impression of intonation, appearance and behaviour. From the interaction of different characters flows the unfolding pattern of events on the stage. Until the reader is familiar with each character, the precise nature of the setting cannot be known. Everyone's home is subtly different. Even impersonal settings mean different things to different people: the warder and the prisoner see the same cell in quite a different light.

The plays in this book have been written to help the process of visualizing performance from text. *They are very short.* They attempt to achieve in miniature what the authors have already achieved at length in their published works. The plays can be read quickly. They can then be studied and read again. Their themes and situations can be improvised, their lines rehearsed — and all in a brief space of time. First Night lies within easy reach of first reading.

Despite the rigour imposed by writing for a playing-time of some ten minutes, the playwrights have made no concessions to the form. The short plays reflect their recurring themes and differing styles. It is interesting that James Saunders and David Selbourne confront the basic ambiguity of theatre in the first of their two plays. Their treatment of it is illuminatingly different as could be expected after reading their individual prefaces. Both N.F. Simpson and Vivienne Welburn touch on group dynamics, although to compare *In Reasonable Shape* with *Snakes and Ladders* in any other respect would be absurd. *And after Nature*, *Art* and *Over the Wall* can perhaps be called parables for our time but they have little else in common. Dramatic forms range from the naturalism in *Vacant Possession* to an absurdist conversation piece like *Anyone's Gums Can Listen to Reason* to the poetic realism of *Think of a Story, Quickly!* and the humorous fantasy of *We Three*. The ten plays present a unique spectrum of the infinite variety inherent in the art of writing for the theatre.

Performed together in any combination, they would provide
opportunities to create individual character studies or experience
what is called 'ensemble' playing; they would challenge the
imagination of directors to respond to the variety of form and to
create a theatrical experience with minimal technical resources;
and they would intrigue, stimulate and entertain audiences of any
age.

R.R.

James Saunders

James Saunders was born in Islington, London in 1925. He was educated at Wembley County School and Southampton University. He was a teacher by day and a playwright by night until devoting all his time to writing. *Next Time I'll Sing to You* ran at the Criterion Theatre in 1963 and since then his plays have enjoyed enormous success both in the West End and with amateur theatre clubs. *A Scent of Flowers*, a play in three acts, was first staged at the Duke of York's in 1964. James Saunders is married and has three children, and lives in Twickenham.

Plays
Barnstable (Hutchinson 1961, French)
Next Time I'll Sing to You (Deutsch 1963, Heinemann 1965,
    Penguin 1971)
Double Double (Blackie 1964, French)
A Scent of Flowers (Deutsch 1965, Heinemann 1968, Penguin 1971)
Neighbours and Other Plays (Deutsch 1968, Heinemann 1968,
    Penguin 1971)
The Italian Girl (Adaptation) (French 1968)
The Borage Pigeon Affair (Deutsch 1970, Penguin 1971)
Travails of Sancho Panza (Heinemann 1970)
A Man's Best Friend (in *Mixed Doubles*, Methuen 1970)
Games and After Liverpool (French 1973)
Act (in *The Fun Art Bus*, Methuen 1973)
Bye Bye Blues (Fringescripts 1973)

'I was driving my car once, and feeling bored, and tried imagining that the car was stationary and the countryside was moving, the road rolling backwards under the wheels like a Test-Your-Driving-Skill machine in an amusement arcade. I noticed that the further I depressed the accelerator pedal, the faster everything whizzed back past me; and if I gave the wheel a right-hand turn the road turned to the left. I felt my co-ordination going. And yet, assuming I was travelling from East to West, with the Earth turning from West to East. . . Still, no point in causing an accident; I gave up the experiment and went back to assuming, like any normal person, that I was moving and the Earth stood still.

In order to drive comfortably through our little space and time (or is it time that's moving in the opposite direction?) without too many accidents, we take a lot of things for granted, leave a lot of

questions unanswered, or unasked. If you ask a machine-operator: "What makes that there wheel go round?" he might say: "Me pushing this here green button" — a fair enough answer if you just want to operate the machine, but not much use for knowing what it's all about. Most of the questions we ask are operator's questions, and the answers we accept are operator's answers.
Q: What happens to me when I die? A: You get shoved into the ground. That's true (unless you are cremated) and sufficient for practical purposes. But if people get to thinking it's a complete answer rather than just an operating instruction, they need to take a holiday from operating their lives and have a good, long, quiet think.

One place to take the holiday is into Art. Art is that region of experience where, because it's not involved in the *machinery* of living, strange questions can be asked and strange answers given. Van Gogh answered the question "What does a sunflower look like?" — but not by taking a photograph. And his answer can't be verbalised, only seen in the painting. Art is non-verbal, in a world which is becoming more and more verbal. (We even now have cold wars, which are verbal wars.) Theatre is non-verbal; it *uses* words, as painters use paint, but what it tries to get at is underneath the words, underneath the logical exposition. Art is a rebellion against the tyranny of life as a mechanical operation. It calls into question the accepted views of the world. This is why despotic regimes and despotic individuals try to censor it. And yet, in fact, Art has no temporal power — no guns, no economic weapons. Theatre is a playspace where you can ask silly or serious questions about life, death, time, space, freedom and compulsion, what it is to see and hear, what words really are. . . It cannot do harm, unless experience is harm. Never trust censors.'

What Theatre Really Is

*Any number can play. But for convenience I
have assumed nine actors, designated by
numbers, and nine members of the audience,
designated by letters. This play was written to
be done in the classroom (though, if you want
to have a go at adapting it for a 'real' stage and
a 'real' audience, you can). The play is
unfinished. What follows, I imagine, is that the
teacher, playing the part of The Teacher,
brilliantly resolves the paradox; this is followed
by an improvised discussion, or argument, or
riot; and the bell goes, or the police are called.*

1: I am an actor.
2: So am I
3: So am I
4: Me too.
5: I wasn't a minute ago.
6: I was just a person.
7: Now I'm an actor. Because I'm on a stage saying lines.
8: Because I'm saying lines this is now a stage. And I'm on it.
9: It wasn't a minute ago.
1: It used to be a bit of the classroom.
2: Not any more. Not now.
3: Behold the stage!
4: Magic.
5: We haven't done anything to it. But it's changed into a stage.
6: Because *we're* on it. And *we're actors!*
7: Because we're on a stage.
8: Saying lines.
9: Because we're actors.
1: Because we're on a stage.
2: Because we're actors.
3: I've always wanted to be an actor.

Pause.

4: That makes *them audience.*

A: That's us.

B: Me.

C: Me.

D: Me too.

E: Me too.

5: They weren't two minutes ago.

6: They are now.

7: Because they're sitting there watching us.

8: Being actors.

9: On a stage.

1: To an audience.

2: Wait a minute. We are actors because an audience is sitting there watching us on a stage saying lines.

3: This is a stage because we are actors saying lines to an audience on it.

4: That's an audience because we're saying lines on a stage to them.

5: That's got that straightened out.

6: This is better than algebra.

7: It's good to know what you are.

Pause.

8: That makes us very important. If it wasn't for us actors there wouldn't be any stage and there wouldn't be any audience.

F: But if it wasn't for the stage there wouldn't be anywhere to be actors *on.*

G: And if it wasn't for us audience there wouldn't be anyone to be actors *to.* Stage or no stage.

H: We're *all terribly important!*

J: Cor!

A: What it is to be needed!

Pause.

9: We're not, though, you know.

1: Not what?

9: Actors. We're not actors.

2: *They're* not.

9: *We're* not.

3: We've done all that. We're actors because this is a stage because there's an audience because we're on a stage because we're actors because there's an audience because . . .

9: No.

4: It's no good saying no. Anyone can say no.

9: Characters.

4: What?

9: An actor on a stage says lines. Plays a character.

5: *Plays* a character?

9: *Becomes* a character.

6: You said plays. *Who* plays the character?

9: The actor.

7: Well then.

9: Well then what?

7: Well then if I'm an actor playing a character then I'm not a character, I'm an *actor*. *Playing* a character.

9: No.

8: It's no good saying no.

9: No, you're a character *being played by* an actor.

1: What's the difference?

9: The difference is you're a character. You're not an actor any more.

2: All right, I'm both.

9: You can't be both. You must be one or the other.

3: All right. I'm *pretending* to be a character. I'm pretending. I'm play-acting. I'm really an actor, but I'm *pretending* to be a *character*.

4: Got you there.

9: Who's pretending?

3: What?

9: Who is it who's pretending?

3: *I* am!

9: Who's that?

3: Me, me! This one here, *me*.

9: That character?

3: No, *me!*

9: But you're saying lines. You're reading lines out of that book.

4: What about it?

9: So they're not your lines. They're somebody else's. Somebody else wrote them. They belong to somebody else. The character. They're the character's lines. The me is the character's me. The me is the character.

3: But I *am* the . . .! I mean I'm pretending to be the . . .

9: Who is?

3: Are you trying to say I don't exist?

9:   Who?

3:   *Me.* The actor.

9:   Which actor? The one in the book who says he's not a character?

3:   I've had enough of this. I'm going to be audience.

6:   This is worse than algebra.

4:   There's always a trouble-maker in any group.

Pause.

1:   I am an actor.

9:   Character.

1:   I am a character.

2:   So am I.

3:   So am I.

4:   Me too.

5:   I wasn't five minutes ago.

6:   I was just an actor.

7:   Now I'm a character. Because I'm on a stage saying my lines.

8:   Not anyone else's. *Mine.* Because I'm saying my lines this is now a stage. Which I'm on.

9:   It wasn't five and a bit minutes ago.

1:   It used to be a bit of the classroom.

2:   It still is.

1:   What?

2:   It still is.

3:   It's a stage.

2:   It's a bit of the classroom.

3:   It's a *stage.*

2:   It's a bit of the classroom.

4:   Look, we've done this. It's a stage. I am an actor . . .

9:   Character.

4:   I am a character saying my lines to an audience, therefore this is a stage. By definition.

2:   No.

5:   You can't say no.

2:   I can say no. An *actor* says lines to an audience on a stage. You're not an actor, you're a *character. Characters* say lines to *each other*, or sometimes to themselves, known as soliloquy, as in "To be or not to be", and they don't say them on a stage but in wherever they're supposed to be in the play when they say them, as it might be a blasted heath or a bloody battlefield or indeed the court of Denmark.

6: Who is this bighead?

7: Another trouble-maker.

8: All right, where *are* the characters supposed to be?

2: In a classroom. Not this one, of course, the one in the play.

6: Come back algebra, all is forgiven.

Pause.

1: I am a character.

2: So am I.

3: So am I.

4: Me too.

5: On a stage.

2: Classroom.

6: In a classroom, though not this one.

7: Saying my lines to the other characters.

8: Or to myself.

9: There is an audience . . .

1: Why can't you be both?

9: What?

1: Why can't you be both? Actor *and* character. Both at the same time.

3: Who let this one in?

1: Why can't you?

4: Yet another trouble-maker.

1: Why can't you?

5: Listen, dolt. Actors are real, right? And characters are not real, right? And you can't be real and not real at the same time, right?

1: Why can't you?

6: Get him off! Kick him out!

7: Trouble-maker!

8: Subversive!

3: Mystic!

4: It's characters like you get the youth of today a bad name.

1: In two different ways. You can be real in one way and unreal in another way. Who says you can't? Or *real* in two different ways. Who says imagination isn't real? Who says you're more real when you're awake than you are when you're dreaming? If you're in bed having a dream what's more real, you lying in bed or your dream? And who says characters can't talk to audiences? And who says . . .?

5: Get rid of this revolutionary!
A: What do you think of it so far?
B: Rubbish.
5: Who said that?
6: Let's have a bit of order.
7: Let's have a bit of structure. Silence for ten seconds.
9: Nine.
8: Eight.
7: That's not silence.

Pause.

7: Right. Now.
1: I am a character.
2: So am I.
3: So am I.
4: Me too.
5: Me also.
6: We used to be persons.
7: And this was a classroom.
8: Then we decided to be actors. We made the big decision.
9: Which turned this into a stage and them into an audience. And then . . .
C: No, we decided to be audience.
5: Who said that?
C: I did. We made the big decision too.
3: No talking in the audience.
D: Why not?
4: Because audiences don't talk.
1: Who says so?
5: You keep out of this. *We* decided to be actors. So we're in charge. What we say goes. You lot didn't decide anything, so you're audience.
E: No.
5: It's no good saying no.
F: I did decide something. I decided not to be an actor.
5: That doesn't count.
1: Who says so?
G: I decided to be audience.
H: I decided not to make any decision.
J: I couldn't decide.
A: I decided not to decide not to be audience.
B: I couldn't care less what I am.
6: No talking in the audience!

C: We're not audience. We're saying lines so we're actors.

D: Characters.

E: On a stage.

7:   You can't do that.

E: We're doing it. Therefore *you're* the audience.

7:   *You're* the audience.

E: *You're* the audience. We're actors.

2:   Characters.

E: Characters.

7:   You're not, you're audience. I'm going to write to the Educational Authority about this. You're undermining the system.

3:   I may as well be an actor again. At least I'll know what I am. I think.

1:   Who says they can't be actors *and* audience? And characters. And . . .

5:   Look, I won't tell you again.

6:   This could lead straight to anarchy.

7:   Five seconds silence!

Pause.

7:   Right.

1:   Once we were persons.

2:   In a classroom.

3:   We knew what we were then. It was nice.

4:   Then we had to go and decide to be actors.

G: And we decided to be audience.

F: Or not to be actors.

H: Or left it to fate, and decided not to decide or didn't decide to decide.

5:   So the classroom turned into a stage.

6:   But as soon as we started being actors by saying lines we stopped being actors and turned into characters.

2:   So we were never actors at all, or only for an infinitesimal fraction of time, as if the straight line of me as a person touched the circle of me as an actor at a tangent and continued as me as a character.

6:   Bighead.

7:   Or we were actors all the time as well as characters.

8:   As well as persons.

J: Meanwhile, back at base-camp, the audience

started saying lines and turned immediately into actors.

2:   Or characters.

1:   Or both.

9:   Which made us audience.

3:   In which case we are all persons and audience and actors and characters.

4:   Meanwhile the classroom had turned into a stage for the actors, back into a classroom for the characters, though not of course the same one . . .

A: And into an auditorium for the audience.

5:   Which is of course us as well.

B: So the classroom is now a stage, an auditorium and two classrooms.

6:   There's some trickery going on somewhere.

3:   I don't like this game. I want to go home.

2:   Perhaps it's a question of semantics. Could we be confusing the objective reality of a ding un zish with the subjective process of apperception? That is the question. If I may quote Wittgenstein . . .

6:   Bighead!

5:   I hate to say this, but I think we need the experience and advice of the older generation on this, tainted though they may be with outdated concepts and reactionary ideas. Teacher!

7:   Help, please.

ALL: Teacher!

Over the Wall

Any number can play. But I have numbered the speeches from one to nine. The narration may be shared out.

N: There was once an island, if you believe it, on which lived a people no better and no worse than most. They had enough to eat, without stuffing themselves, everyone had a day's work (which in those times was considered a great blessing), the old were looked after, as long as they didn't outstay their welcome, and the young were respected as individuals — within reason. All this had been so for as long as anyone could remember, and so they hoped it would continue. For, while they were not exactly happy they were not exactly unhappy either. And as they said to each other when they bothered to talk about it:

1: If it was good enough for my father it's good enough for me. That's what my father used to say, and it's what I say too.

2: Absolutely. Leave well alone, that's my motto.

3: We should count our blessings. It's better than it was in the bad old days.

4: Mind you, it's not so good as it was in the good old days.

5: But things could always be worse. That's what we should think of.

6: They could always be better, of course.

5: But they could always be worse.

7: At least we're allowed to work all day.

8: And we're allowed not to work on Saturday and Sunday.

9: And we've got the vote. We didn't have that in the bad old days.

6: *(female)* We didn't have it in the good old days.

N: So they counted their blessings and rested content. Now what made this island different

from any other you might have in mind was a
wall, which ran across the island a bit more than
halfway down and which had been there as long
as anyone could remember, and as long as
anyone they could remember could remember.
For ever, in fact, as far as they knew or cared.
They called it 'The Wall', and if they ever
talked about it they said things like:

1:   There's always been a Wall and there always will
be, that's the way things are. It's a fact of
nature. There's nothing you can do about it.

2:   There must be a purpose in it, that's what I say.
Everything has its purpose: wars, walls, it's all
meant.

3:   There are things beyond us. A higher Wall, I
mean Will. Someone's in charge up there. The
great Wall-Builder in the sky. He knows what's
best for us. Leave it to Him, that's what I say.

6:   Or Her.

4:   After all, when you think of us — human beings
— crawling on the earth . . . I mean humility's
called for. It's not for us to seek to understand
the sublime purpose.

5:   *Of* which the Wall is part.

4:   *Of* which the Wall is part.

1:   It was good enough for my father, and it's good
enough for me. That's what my father used to
say. Leave it at that. Nuff said.

N: So they went on with their business, working,
as they were allowed to, through the week, and
on Saturdays and Sundays working, as they
were allowed to, at what they called their leisure
activities. This wall, now, was not quite straight
but curved outwards, so that you could never
see the two ends of it together. Not that it had
ends, for as the fishermen knew, it continued,
when it reached the sea, back along both shores
to meet itself again at the far end of the island,
so encircling the half of it — a bit more than
half.

7:   Lor, Jarge, yon Wall goos roit raind the oisland.

8:   Oi knoos thaat, Taam. Tis a well-knoon faact.

N: So they spoke when they fished. High it was,
and smooth, and impregnable, and how it got
there no one knew. There were theories, of
course.

9:   There is no doubt that it was constructed in the

Neo-plasticene Age by primitive tree-worshippers,
to enclose the sacred grove of the earth-goddess . . .

1:   It was built of course, by invading Venusians,
as a navigational aid and to protect the space-
ships from marauding dinosaurs.

2:   Obviously a natural outcrop of rock, pushed up
by volcanic activity and then worn smooth by
the wind and rain, an interesting
phenomenomenom.

3:   It's a figment of the imagination. The Wall only
exists in our minds. If we stopped thinking it
was there it wouldn't be.

N: No one could prove this theory wrong.

4:   I walked into it last night in the dark. Look at
the bump on my forehead.

3:   Psychosomatic. You *imagined* it was there, so
when you got to where you imagined it was
you walked into it and imagined you hurt
yourself. It stands to reason.

4:   It still hurts.

3:   You think it does.

N: But since it seemed to make not much
difference, if you thought you walked into it,
whether you were really hurt or only thought
you were, people tried not to. Except for one
poor fellow who so convinced himself that the
wall was imaginary that he took a flying leap
at where it was, or wasn't, and dashed his brains
out. Or so it seemed.

5:   Excuse me, I'm conducting a survey. May I ask
what *you* think is on the other side of the Wall?

6:   I don't want to talk about it. I think it's
disgusting. There's enough nasty *this* side of the
Wall, never mind the *other* side of the Wall.

7:   It's like a beautiful garden, with fruit hanging
down and bambis and pretty flowers. And you
don't have to wear any clothes.

8:   It's like a sort of a ooze, a sort of — like a —
ooze, sort of.

9:   Nothing.

5:   Nothing?

9:   Nothing. Everything finishes at the Wall. Then
there's nothing.

1:   The fifth dimension.

2:   Ethereal vibrations.

3:   That is to say, beyond the Wall the laws of
space-time as we know them no longer operate.

Call it ethereal vibrations, call it the fifth
dimension, call it a rolypoly pudding . . .

1: In other words, as far as we're concerned it
doesn't exist in there — if one can say "in there"
for a "there" which doesn't exist and therefore
cannot be said to be either *in* or *there*. As for
what doesn't exist . . .

3: It's like a mathematical point really . . .

9: Like I said, nothing.

2: Don't know.

3: Don't know.

4: Don't know.

6: Don't care.

N: So there it was. Or wasn't, or was in a different
way, or seemed to be.

1: Mum!

2: What?

1: What's over the Wall?

2: You wash your mouth out with soapy water! I'll
give you over the Wall! Wait till I tell your father!

3: Dad!

4: What?

3: What's over the Wall?

4: Ask your teacher. What d'you think I pay rates
and taxes for? To teach you myself?

3: I asked my teacher.

4: Well?

3: Said to get on with my algebra.

4: Well, then, do what your teacher says.

3: But what *is* over the Wall?

4: The toe of my boot. Get on with your homework.

3: I've done my homework. What *is* over the — ?

4: Then do something else. Can't you see I'm
trying to watch telly?!

N: Or whatever it was they watched in those days;
it wasn't telly.

4: Can't you see I'm trying to watch the goldfish?

5: Can't you see I'm trying to get this ferret out of
my trousers?

6: Can't you see I'm trying to invent the wheel?

7: — cook the joint?

8: — bath the baby?

9: — darn my socks?

4: — frame a photo of my mother?

5: — write a sonnet?

6: — make a fortune?

7:   — get my head out from between these railings?

8:   — bury the cat?

9:   — dig a well starting at the bottom?

N: Or whatever. And so, in short, on the whole, more or less, without splitting hairs, broadly speaking, in a nutshell, they ignored it.

1:   Pretended it wasn't there.

N: Well, no, they couldn't do that. Because it was. No, they just . . . ignored it; as you might ignore a gatecrasher at a party whom nobody knows and nobody wants to, who turns up in the wrong gear with a nasty look on his face and what looks like a flick-knife sticking out of one pocket. All except one.

3:   It's ridiculous.

2:   What is?

3:   It's stupid. I can't believe it. It's ludicrous. Here we are with a great Wall across the island and we don't even know why and no one seems to care.

2:   It's not for us mere mortals to ask why.

3:   Why not?

2:   Because we're mere mortals, that's why not.

3:   I'm not a mere mortal, I'm a rational human being.

5:   We're not meant to understand everything, you know.

3:   Why not, who says so?

6:   There's enough needs putting right *this* side of the Wall, never mind the *other* side of the Wall.

7:   Get on with your work and think yourself lucky. Thinking about the Wall won't do you any good.

8:   Do some leisure activities, take your mind off it. Do some healthy outdoor pursuits.

4:   All you do is talk about the Wall. Wall, Wall, Wall, that's all I get from you.

2:   Leave wall alone, I mean leave well alone, that's my advice.

1:   Ignorance was good enough for your father and it ought to be good enough for you.

4:   Who do you think you are anyway? God or somebody?

3:   I want to know what's on the other side!!

5:   Next please. Well, now, what seems to be the matter with you?

3:   I'm having a bit of trouble, doctor.

5:   What sort of trouble? Stick out your tongue.

3: It'th athout the Thall . . .

5: Put your tongue in.

3: It's about the Wall. All I want to know . . .

5: Bowel movements all right?

3: Yes, thanks. All I want to know is what's on the other side, that seems reasonable enough to me, only —

5: Sleeping all right, are you? Getting the old beauty sleep?

3: I dream about walls. Only no one else seems to be bothered, only me, so I —

5: How's your sex-life? Sex-life all right, is it? The old nudge nudge wink wink?

3: I'm not bothered, thanks. So I wondered if there's something wrong with me, or if in fact —

5: Eating all right, are you? Getting the old nosh down?

3: Yes, I'm eating. Or if in fact it's that there's something wrong with everybody else. And it's turning into a bit of —

5: How's the pains in the leg? Pains in the leg all right?

3: They're fine. Into a bit of an obsession. Because, I mean, you don't just ignore something like that, I mean I'm not a mere mortal I'm a rational human being and it could be important, I mean, *look* at the flaming thing, I mean *look* at it, there it is, look, there!

5: Any neuralgia, headache, backache, loss of breath, vomiting, congenital idiocy, piles, trouble with the waterworks, spots before the eyes, dizzy spells?

3: D — I — Z — Z —

5: Falling hair, loss of weight, gain of weight, tenseness, got a drink problem have you, smoking too much, hallucinations, palpitations, eructations, on drugs are you, can you read the top line, overdoing it at work perhaps, worrying about the work, about the spouse, about where to go for your holiday, about the mortgage, about the value of the pound, about the political situation, about your old mother, about the kids, kids playing you up are they, not doing well at school, got a drink problem have they, smoking, on drugs are they, suffering from loss of weight, falling hair, got any worries have you?

3: Yes!

5:   Have you seen a priest?

3:   Yes. She didn't know either.

5:   Didn't know what? They're not supposed to know, they're supposed to give comfort. Seen a psychiatrist, have you, consulted a shrink?

3:   He said it was my mother.

5:   Well there you are. Here's a prescription. Take some four times a day, and if there's any left over rub it on your chest. Or your mother's chest. I don't care.

3:   What's wrong with me, doctor?

5:   You're a nut. Get out, you're wasting my time.

N: So out he got, this nut, taking his obsession with him, and the doctor turned thankfully to the next patient, a nice simple case who'd put his thumb out trying to plant beans in hard ground.

5:   Put your thumb out, have you? How's your bowel movements? Sleeping all right?

3:   I'm going to start an Association for Investigating The Wall In Order To See What's On The Other Side. The AFITWIOTSWOTOS. Catchy title. They'll flock to join. Then we'll get somewhere.

N: But they didn't. And after a while he disbanded the association, with the full agreement of the members — himself. But he didn't give up.

3:   All right. I'm on my own. So be it. But I'm going to find out what's on the other side of That Wall. If it kills me.

N: And for the next thirty or forty years he did nothing but think about the Wall. He read books, consulted sages, took measurements, drew diagrams, worked out theories, studied history, biology, theology, psychology, astrology, cogitated, meditated and did a bit of yoga on the side. He lost his friends of course.

6:   Oh, don't invite *him*. He'll only talk about the Wall.

N: His marriage went for a Burton.

4:   Wall, Wall, Wall, nothing but Wall! I'm sick of Wall! And I'm sick of you too! I'm going home to father!

N: Slam. His kids turned delinquent.

7:   What are you doing tonight?

8:   Thought I'd cripple a few fuzz.

7:   We did that last night.

N: Until finally, old, alone and penniless, he decided on the direct approach, and built his great invention: a sort of a catapult, quite novel in those times, which could hurl an object, or a person, up to an enormous height. He tried it on a rock, which disappeared into the blue, and then, one day, surrounded by curious bystanders, sat his own skinny, threadbare old body where the rock had been.

3:    Wind it up, then.

N: They did.

3:    When I say three, pull the lever. One . . . two . . . thr . . . ooww!

N: They did, only too glad to get rid of this nut, this disruptive influence, so they could get back to watching their goldfish and planting their beans.

9:    There he goes!

1:    Look at his rags flapping!

2:    Bald head glinting in the sun!

4:    Better than fireworks!

5:    Coo!

N: Up he went, up, up, up, until looking down . . . we surmise . . . he saw the whole gold of that sunny day, the whole spread of the earth and seas, saw the tiny moving figures of people and the infinite distances of space. And it looked good.

3:    I'm up! I'm over! I can see! I can see over! It's. . . It's . . . It's . . . Aaah!

N: A heart attack — we surmise. But in any case he was too far away for those on the ground to hear him. And as he dwindled into what seemed like a mathematical point, and disappeared, those on the ground shook their heads, or giggled, and went back to their beans, and their goldfish.

David Selbourne

David Selbourne was born in London in 1937, educated at
Manchester Grammar School and Balliol College, Oxford, trained
as a lawyer and is now a tutor in political theory at Ruskin College,
Oxford. His first full length play, *The Play of William Cooper and
Edmund Dew-Nevett* was first staged in 1968 at the Northcott
Theatre, Exeter, and *The Two-Backed Beast* was staged in
December, 1968 at the Everyman Theatre, Liverpool. *Dorabella*
was first staged at the Traverse Theatre, Edinburgh, in October,
1969.

Plays
The Play of William Cooper and Edmund Dew-Nevett (Methuen
    1968)
The Two-Backed Beast (Methuen 1969)
Dorabella (Methuen 1970)
The Damned (Methuen 1971)
Samson and Alison Mary Fagan (Calder & Boyars 1971)
Class Play (Hutchinson Playbill 1973)

Other Works
An Eye to China (Black Liberator Press 1975)
An Eye to India (Penguin Books 1977)

'The theatrical form has its demands and its limitations, the
theatrical mode its point (and pointlessness), but they are
not governed by the age of the actors or the audience. Thus, these
two short plays ask and seek to answer — because every question
has an answer — the same questions that I have asked in my other
work for the theatre. And if the actors are young, the questions
are older; and they can be understood by everybody, and asked by
anyone who wants to.

   They are games to play also; whoever acts in them, produces
them and watches them should remember that. So, if they have
any depths, they should not be sought out, not striven for, as if
life depended upon it. Life depends on other things and other
people, and not upon the life of the theatre, or the people who
inhabit it, however beguiling; and somewhere in these two plays,
I believe that that is said also.

   Finally, the plays are directed outwards; they are not plays of
introspection. They are concerned with relations; between the

actors themselves, between the actors and the school-world which is their setting, between the actor and the writer, and between actors, writer and the society we inhabit. The compass of a few minutes, a few pages, a few people is small, but sufficient to suggest and place these relations.

I do not make any distinction between my work for the theatre and my other writing. The preoccupations, the themes and the forms are common to both. Whatever I have learned from always insufficient production of my work for the theatre has been turned to prose writing; something of it may have been compressed into these two short plays. I look forward to their performance and, if invited, will try to come and see them.'

What's Acting?

*JOHN, KATE and FRED, three fourteen-or
fifteen-year-olds; in school. There are eight
short scenes.*

One

John: There's no point in acting.
What's the point of acting?

A pause.

In this zoo.
Kate: There is a point in acting.
It's so . . . tell him . . . I dunno, Fred, it's sort
of . . .
Feeling . . .
Fred: Feeling?
Feeling's not acting.
Feeling's just feeling.
Kate: I dunno.
It's sort of . . . acting.
Fred: *(mocking)* It's . . . it's . . . you know . . . drama.
(kissing sound) Romantic.
John: It's just messing.
Sucking up to teachers.
Creeping.
Kate: What are you doing now then?
If you're so clever.
Eh, clever?
What are you doing?

A pause.

John: I'm not acting.
I'm talking,
I'm only talking.
Kate: That's acting.
I mean what's acting,
If it isn't talking?
I mean, talking's acting,

And acting's talking.
You know what I mean.
It's only natural . . .

John: *(mocking)* . . . and just keep walking, that's all,
And posing.

Fred: If you're not acting,
What are you doing then, exactly,
If you're not acting?

John: I'm not acting,
I'm just speaking,
And walking;
Sort of talking.

Fred: *(to Kate)* He's acting.

Silence.

Two

John: It's so boring.
They got jobs in it.

Fred: Yeah.

Kate: Jobs in what?

John: Talking.

Fred: And walking.

John: They got jobs in it,
Degrees,
It's only part of English,
Sort of elocution,
It isn't serious,
It's just messing.

Fred: Filling time.

John: Fooling us.

Fred: Keeping us quiet.

John: Like spelling.

Fred: Or dictation.

Kate: You must be joking.

John: Jobs in it.
Teaching talking.

Fred: Teaching walking.

Laughter.

Three

John: *(posing)* It's just money for nothing.
Waste of money.

Kate: You're acting now, John, honest.
Really well; really,
Isn't he?

Sort of putting it all on,
That's acting.

Fred: Putting on an act,
That's acting.

Kate: Go on then,
Prove you're not acting,
If you're not acting.

Fred: Go on, prove it.

John: I'm going.
And I mean it.
That's not acting,
That's not 'movement',
That's just going,
If I'm going.

Kate: Go on then.

Fred: Push off then,
If you're going.
Who cares whether you're acting?

Kate: Who cares whether you're acting,
Or not acting,
Who cares about it?

John: OK, I'm going.

Fred: See, he's shamming.
He's not going.
He's acting.

John: Shamming isn't acting.

Fred: What is it then,
If shamming isn't acting?

John: Acting's acting.
Shamming's shamming,
Messing.
I'm going.

Kate: You're not going.
You're only pretending.

Fred: He's acting. He isn't going.

Four

Kate: They're watching.
So you must be acting.

John: Just because they're watching,
Doesn't mean I'm acting.

Fred: O yes, it does.

John: I can act any time,
If I want.
If I want,
I can act any time.

Fred: Speak for yourself, mate,

Call that acting?

John: But I don't want to,
Not with them watching,
Not with them forcing, teaching,
Teaching walking,
Teaching talking,
Because they've got jobs in it.

Fred: You've got to.

John: *(aggressive)* Who says I've got to?!

Fred: They do.

John: *(softly)* Who are they then?

Silence.

Five

Kate: *(sweetly)* You said you wanted to.
You said you did.
You put your hand up.
You asked to.
You know it.

Fred: Sucking.

Kate: Remember? You said . . .

John: Not forcing.
Not in lessons.

Fred: How can it be forcing . . .

Kate: When you asked to . . .

Fred: How can it be forcing?

John: If I want to,
When I want to!
Not forcing.

Fred: Who's forcing?

Kate: You're good at it.
You . . . sort of . . .
I dunno how to explain it . . .

A pause.

John: They're using it.
I can feel it.

Fred: You're barmy.

John: It's not acting.

Kate: Go on with you,
What is it,
If it isn't acting,
If it isn't acting,
What is it?

John: Using us, messing.

Silence.

Six

Kate: You're very suspicious,
Really, John,
You are, suspicious really,
You're very peculiar,
Really, John,
You oughtn't.

John: Acting, learning lines.
Prancing around,
Pretending, play-acting.

Fred: *(shouting)* You've learned 'em,
You've learned these 'uns,
You liar!!
So what are you doing?!!

Kate: You learned them,
You didn't have to,
You learned them . . .

Fred: You're speaking them,
So who are you kidding?!!

John: I'm not lying,
I mean it.

Fred: You didn't write 'em,
So who are you kidding,
You mean it,
What do you mean exactly?
You didn't write 'em!!

Kate: They're not even your feelings.

Fred: *(pointing at a script)* They're his feelings.

Kate: He wrote 'em.
You haven't got any feelings.

A pause.

(sweetly) You're just acting.
Like we told you.

Fred: You couldn't say anything at all,
If you hadn't learned it.

Kate: *(poshly)* You'd just be speechless,
With your mouth open,
Just gormless;
Someone like you.
Gormless.

Seven

John: *(to Fred)* I've got plenty to say,
Without being told, mate,
Plenty.

                I've got my own ideas,
                And I'm going to say them,
                One day.

Kate: Listen who's talking.

John: *(to Fred)* I don't need a script, mate,
                Speak for yourself, mate.
                And it won't need acting, either.
                They're using us,
                The lot of 'em,
                To stop us speaking,
                Speaking what they tell us . . .

Fred: *(aside)* . . . sucking . . .

John: I'm acting this once,
                But it's the last time,
                Next time,
                I'll do the speaking,
                With my own voice,
                And my own words,
                I'll do the speaking.

Kate: Listen who's talking.

Fred: *(to audience)* He learned that, and all.

Kate: John, you're a good actor.

John: There's no point in acting.
                What's the point of acting?

A silence.

                There is none. Not in this zoo.
                Not with this stuff, I'll tell you.
                I could do better with my eyes shut.

Fred: Go on then, try it.

Eight

Kate: He wrote that as well.

A pause.

                Who is he?

John: That's not the point.

Kate: He wrote that as well, didn't he,
                'That's not the point,'
                He wrote it, not you, and you say it,
                So why don't you stop it,
                I could scream,
                It's getting so boring.

Fred: He wrote it, but we said it.

John: And if we say it, we can change it.

Kate: *(shouting)* He wrote that as well, didn't he?
He wrote it!! Every word you're speaking!!
Every word I'm speaking! It's madness!

Fred: Nobody can make us.

Kate: *(pleading)* But he wrote that, not you, Fred.

A pause.

John: Only to tell us.

Kate: Tell us what, I don't get it!

John: To tell us,
There's no point in acting,
That's what,
Not in this zoo, there isn't.

A pause.

I told you,
At the beginning.

Think of a Story, Quickly!

JANE, KATHY, and LOUISA, three girls of thirteen or fourteen; in school. There is one scene only.

Kathy: She said, think of a story, quickly!

Groans.

Jane: Act it.
Kathy: She's barmy.
Jane: She said, pretend you're a tree, or something.
Kathy: *(gesticulating)* Or a monkey.
   (gesturing) Feel it in your branches!

Laughter.

Jane: School's so boring.
   I can't stand it.
Louisa: I don't mind it.
Kathy: I can't stand it.

A pause.

Louisa: Going out tonight?
Jane: No.
Kathy: No.
Jane: Are you?
Louisa: Yes.
Kathy: Where to?
Louisa: Dunno yet.

A pause.

Kathy: Who with, then?

Giggles.

Louisa: Nosey-parker, you are.
Kathy: I was only asking.

Jane:	Who is it, tell us. Go on, tell us!
Louisa:	What do you want to know for?
Jane:	Because.
Louisa:	Because what?
Jane:	Because.
Kathy:	Oo, mysterious!

A pause.

Louisa:	Freddie.

Giggles.

Jane:	Him?
	You must be joking.
Kathy:	Him?!
Louisa:	He's not bad looking.

Giggles.

Jane:	You're blushing!
	Why are you blushing?
Kathy:	She's getting redder!
Louisa:	I'm not getting redder!
Jane:	You are, then.
Kathy:	Isn't it romantic!

Giggles.

Jane:	What are you going to do then?
Kathy:	Where are you going?
Jane:	Do you really like him?
	I think he's awful.
Kathy:	So do I. I think he's awful.
Louisa:	He's not bad looking.

A pause.

Jane:	Do you love him?

Screams and giggles, pushing each other.

Kathy:	Do you love him?
	I bet she loves him.
Jane:	That's why she's blushing.
Kathy:	Do you love him? Why are you blushing?
	Tell us. Go on, tell us.

Giggles.

Louisa:	He's all right.
Jane:	I think he's awful.
Kathy:	He's revolting.
Jane:	He's not bad looking,
	Sometimes.
Louisa:	He's quite good looking.

A pause.

Jane:	Where are you going?
Louisa:	Dunno yet.

A pause.

Kathy:	Think of a story, quickly,
	She'll be back any minute.

A pause.

Jane:	School's so boring.
	I can't stand it.
Kathy:	I don't mind it.
Jane:	I can't stand it.

A silence.

Louisa:	I got this nail just right,
	Now it's broken.
Jane:	How d'you do it?
Kathy:	It makes you spit.
Louisa:	Just when it was getting real long,
	It's broken.
	You wouldn't believe it.
Jane:	. . . when you want to grow it.
Louisa:	Just when you want it to grow,
	It gets broken.
Kathy:	I know.

A pause.

Jane:	Where are you going?
Louisa:	Dunno yet. Haven't decided.

A pause.

Jane: I don't know what you can see in him,
Really.
Can you, Kathy?
Kathy: Not really.
Jane: He's so thin.
Kathy: And he's got dandruff.
Jane: And acne.
Kathy: And he's stupid.
Jane: He's wet.

A pause.

Kathy: If he asked me,
No thank you! Not me.
Never.
Jane: He's always staring.
Staring, staring, staring.
Kathy: I don't know what you can see in him,
I can't, can you?
Jane: You must be stupid.

Laughter.

Kathy: 'Course, she loves him.
Jane: That must be it, then,
Stars in her eyes,
All romantic,
Can't see his pimples, not now he's asked you,
Can you?
Louisa: I quite like him.
Jane: Birds of a feather.
Kathy: He's got no feathers.

Laughter.

Jane: He hasn't grown 'em yet, he hasn't.
Come on, we got to think of a story, quickly.
You heard her.
Act it.
Kathy: *(mocking)* She quite likes him.
Quite a lady.
Jane: Gone all swanky.
Kathy: Only asked us if we were going out,
So you could tell us.
Jane: Typical.
Kathy: Makes you sick.

A pause.

Jane:	Only asked us,
	So you could tell us.
Kathy:	Didn't you?
Jane:	Eh?
Kathy:	Go on, admit it!
Jane:	That's why you asked us,
	Isn't it?
Kathy:	So you could tell us.
Jane:	No other reason, was there?
Kathy:	Only boasting.

A pause.

Jane:	Your little Freddie!
Kathy:	You can keep him.
Jane:	They can keep each other.
Kathy:	You're welcome. They're welcome to each other.
Jane:	Only asked us, so you could tell us.
Kathy:	Doesn't it make you sick?
Jane:	She always made me sick.
	Showing off, swanking.
	Look at me this, look at me that,
	Freddie and Louisa.
	And catty with it.
Kathy:	Serves you right.
Jane:	Everybody hates you, Louisa, we hate you,
	You might as well know it!
Louisa:	I don't care.
	Hate me.
	If you want to,
	Hate me.

A pause.

	He's quite charming, really.
	I like him.
	He likes me.
	I don't mind you calling me,
	You're only jealous.
Jane:	Jealous?
	Of you? Who wants a twit like him?
Kathy:	You must be joking.
	Think of a story, quickly!

A pause.

Jane:	What have we got to be jealous of?
Kathy:	You must be very stuck up,
	To say we're jealous.
Jane:	You fancy yourself, don't you!
Kathy:	Quite charming.
	O, lah-de-dah.
	'He likes me.' Jealous!
	How do you know he likes you?
Jane:	Has he told you?
Kathy:	Has he kissed you?

Giggles, and pushing.

Jane:	Lovey-dovey?
Kathy:	You'll catch his acne.
Jane:	You'll go all spotty,
	If you touch him.
Louisa:	It's nothing serious; we're not going steady.
Jane:	You will, I bet you.
	I can see it.
Kathy:	I can just see you.

A pause.

Louisa:	She'll be back soon.
Jane:	Think of something, Louisa,
	She'll be back in a minute.

A pause.

Kathy:	She can't think of anything.

A pause.

	Only Freddie.
Louisa:	O you!
	Leave off now.

A pause.

Jane:	We're supposed to think of something, Kathy . . .
	I dunno.
	Be something.

A pause.

Kathy:	How can we be something,
	If we aren't anything?
Louisa:	Speak for yourself.

A pause.

Jane:	She's coming.
Louisa:	So what?
Kathy:	We're supposed to be something.
	What can we be?
Louisa:	Anything.
Jane:	I don't get you.
Louisa:	'Course not.
	Too busy moaning.
	'Course not.
Jane:	Oh yes?
Louisa:	Yes.

A pause.

Jane:	School's so boring.
	I can't stand it.
Louisa:	I don't mind it.
Kathy:	I can't stand it.

A pause.

Louisa:	Pretend you're a tree, or something.
Jane:	Or a monkey.
Kathy:	What happens after? After all this play-acting . . .
Jane:	. . . Nothing.
Louisa:	Plenty.
Kathy:	Nothing.
Jane:	Nothing.
Louisa:	Plenty.
Jane:	Oh, yeah?
Louisa:	Yes.
Kathy:	Oh, yes?
Jane:	Such as?

A pause.

Louisa:	I'm going out tonight, anyway.
Jane:	Is that all you think of?
Louisa:	No.

Kathy: What else do you think of?
            Nothing!
Louisa: Plenty.

A pause.

Jane: *(whispering)* She's coming.
Kathy: We were supposed to . . .
Jane: *(to Louisa)* It's your fault,
            With that Freddie . . .
Kathy: Talking.
Jane: She said, think of a story.

A pause.

Louisa: I can't think of anything.
Jane: I can't.
Kathy: I can't either.
Jane: Tell her you got a lot on your mind.
Kathy: Yeah, tell her.
Jane: That'll keep her quiet.
Kathy: You want advice. About Freddie.
            She'll love it.
Jane: She'll say,
            'Louisa, later,
            Can't it keep till later?'
Kathy: Say, 'I must know, Miss,
            It's important.
            It can't keep, Miss.'
Jane: 'I must know now, Miss Slater,
            Honest.'
Kathy: 'I'm going out tonight with Freddie,
            I got to know first, Miss.'

Laughter.

Jane: 'Come to my room, Louisa,
            And talk to me in private.'

Laughter; a pause.

Kathy: I don't know what you see in him,
            Honest.

A pause.

Jane:	She said, think of a story,
	And act it.
Louisa:	We have done.
Kathy:	You must be joking.
Louisa:	We acted.
Jane:	You did.
Kathy:	*(to Louisa)* You mean, you did.
Louisa:	So did you.
	You acted.

A pause.

Jane:	Never.
Kathy:	That wasn't acting.

A pause.

Jane:	Think of a story!
Kathy:	Quickly! She's coming!

N.F. Simpson

N.F. Simpson was born in London in 1919, and educated at Emanuel School and the University of London. During the war he served in the Royal Artillery and the Intelligence Corps, and then became a teacher. *A Resounding Tinkle* was first produced at the Royal Court Theatre in 1957 and this was followed by several other successful plays, including *One Way Pendulum* (1959) and *The Cresta Run* (1965). Mr Simpson has also written a radio play, a number of television plays and, in 1976, a novel: *Harry Bleachbaker*. He is married with one daughter.

Plays
A Resounding Tinkle (Faber 1958)
One Way Pendulum (Faber 1960)
The Hole and Other Plays and Sketches (Faber 1964)
The Cresta Run (Faber 1966)
Was He Anyone (Faber 1973)

Novel
Harry Bleachbaker (Harrap 1976)

'N.F. Simpson is a somewhat taciturn Londoner who was born, totally without warning and while looking the other way, in 1919. Uncertain as to what was expected of him, he quickly decided, after forcing himself to one brink after another only to find them towering up in front of him, that the best course was to shrug his shoulders and wait for the brink to come to him. In the meantime, having heard it said that, barring accidents, the earth can support life for another twelve hundred thousand million years, he has devoted himself to the problem of how the human race is to keep itself occupied for all that time. It will have to be got through somehow. One will be able to poke things, and pick things up, and put them down; or distinguish between one thing and another, or between one group of things and another larger, or smaller, group; or between several smaller or larger groups; or one can decide things such as whether to decide oneself or leave it to someone else to decide; and there are trigonometry, eating, travel, counter-espionage, and innumerable other activities, from giving massage to the exercise of magnanimity, which will be competing for those brief moments of leisure when we are not translating poems, torturing people, timing eggs, weeping for the past, heating glue, designing practical joke sets and whistling Land of My Fathers.

Besides fighting, each according to his bent, some for freedom, some for the suppression of freedom, there are logs to be chopped, treaties to be signed, people to be snubbed, walls to be white-washed and Harpic to be sprinkled. In the unlikely event that we should run out of things to pass the time with, there is always just moving about; there is an infinity of speeds that we can choose to move about at. It is the contemplation of all this richness and diversity that more than anything determines the form and content of Mr Simpson's work, which is in fact not his at all, but on loan from a little old lady in Dunstable who wishes to remain anonymous, and whose spelling Mr Simpson has taken it upon himself to correct wherever necessary.

Mr Simpson, whose left foot is slightly the larger of the two, turns the scales at around twelve stone.'

In Reasonable Shape

Characters

Mr Wakefield	Schoolmaster. Fifties.
Mrs Bridgnorth	Housewife and former Civil Servant. Fifties.
Mrs Sinclair	Businesswoman. Forties.
Miss Dacre	Golfing friend of Mrs Sinclair. Forties.
Mr Driscoll	Systems analyst. Thirties.
Miss Huxley	Smartly dressed Oxbridge don. Thirties.

All six characters are together as delegates to a conference from a branch of MENSA, which is a society of people from all walks of life who happen to have a higher than average intelligence. Here, however, they are relaxing from the rigours of debate and engaging in light conversation.

The six characters are sitting at small marble-topped tables on the terrace of a hotel in some Mediterranean country. It is a hot, clear, sunny day and the view is breathtaking. There are more tables than people, and the characters are spread out over the terrace. They are enjoying a mid-morning break from conference, and are chatting as they sit with coffee and tea and soft drinks. The conversation is between people who know one another through having met here, perhaps the day before, and it is of that generalised kind that seems to float in the air, being picked up by this person or that, so it is rare for any one person either to address another directly, or answer another directly. There is a degree of stylisation about it, but none of the characters should give the least indication that they are aware of it.

There are two groupings. There is the grouping on which we go up, and the grouping after they have changed their positions roughly half-way through the play. In the first grouping, MRS SINCLAIR and MISS DACRE share a table downstage right; MR WAKEFIELD and MRS BRIDGNORTH share a table upstage centre; MR DRISCOLL sits alone at a table slightly downstage of them left; and MISS HUXLEY sits alone at a table slightly downstage of MR DRISCOLL left centre. Other tables are placed amongst them. In the second grouping, MRS BRIDGNORTH and MISS HUXLEY occupy the table downstage right; MR DRISCOLL and MRS SINCLAIR share the table upstage centre; MISS DACRE sits alone at a table upstage left centre; and MR WAKEFIELD sits alone at a table downstage left.

MR DRISCOLL brings an envelope from his pocket and, taking his time, opens it and takes out a letter. He unfolds it, looks quickly through it, and then reads it aloud from the beginning.

Driscoll: I am writing from the Equator to ask for your help and advice. This is, as you probably know, one of the hottest places in the world, and I have been sent here by my family to cool my heels for a time.

Mrs Sinclair, as though aware of what follows from long experience of this kind of letter, utters the next phrase before MR DRISCOLL can.

Mrs Sinclair: To my dismay, however . . .

She has divined it correctly, and MR DRISCOLL continues with the letter.

Driscoll: To my dismay . . . though perhaps not surprisingly in view of the temperature . . . it is proving well-nigh impossible to do this.

MR WAKEFIELD picks up the next phrase from what is coming to seem a fairly standard type of letter.

Wakefield:	No sooner am I able to get one heel reasonably cool . . .
Driscoll:	. . . than the other is as hot as ever again. *(He skims over a few lines and continues)* Perhaps I am making a mistake in trying to cool them one at a time.
Miss Dacre:	*(Undertone)* Mistake!
Driscoll:	I should be immensely grateful for your help and advice etcetera as I cannot return home until they are cool and do not want to be stuck here for ever. And then there's a postscript. I would certainly prefer, if possible, to do them both at once, as this would save time. P.P.S. It also occurs to me that once I could well and truly master the art of cooling my own heels in this sort of climate, there would be nothing to stop me going on to cool other people's.
Mrs Sinclair:	He wants to run before he can walk.
Wakefield:	On the other hand, he's not without a sense of responsibility . . . a disposition to look ahead and a concern for his own and other people's future.
Miss Huxley:	Not everyone has either the time or the inclination to cool their own heels, especially if it presents difficulties. Here is someone willing to have a go at doing it for them.
Mrs Bridgnorth:	With their permission.
Miss Dacre:	It would be an effrontery to attempt to do it without.
Driscoll:	He goes on over the page . . . I thought if I could set up in business, I might really be able to do well, and even perhaps open up a while-you-wait service which, if successful, would make my fortune and so render me independent of my family.
Miss Huxley:	It is not unknown for a person or persons whose object it is to reduce the temperature of their heels to dangle them in a mangrove swamp. If one can dangle one's own in this way, there would be surely nothing to stop one similarly dangling other people's.
Wakefield:	For a suitable fee.
Mrs Bridgnorth:	To dangle one's feet in a mangrove swamp would be to invite trouble from crocodiles.
Miss Dacre:	If so be that crocodiles inhabit mangrove swamps.
Miss Huxley:	They do, but not in any numbers.
Driscoll:	*(from letter)* At all events, I should, as I say, be

grateful for any advice you can give. Thanking you in advance . . . etcetera.

There is a pause before MR WAKEFIELD begins to produce extempore a draft answer.

Wakefield: Cooling one's heels is an art. It is an art to which a great many people have devoted many lifetimes and can still not be considered experts. As Seneca said, quoting Hippocrates, in the first century A.D., Ars longa, vita brevis. Or, as Chaucer expressed it for us, The life so short, the craft so long to learn. It must be apparent to you, there-fore, that you are proposing to embark on a task which is going to be far from easy . . .

Miss Huxley: Prove.

Wakefield: . . . prove far from easy, and I must disabuse you of any expectation to the contrary.

Mrs Sinclair: There are no short cuts to excellence.

Wakefield: When, after a lifetime of studious application, you reach a point where you can with some approximation to expertise cool your own heels more or less adequately, any attempt, however well-intentioned, to cool the heels of others is not only foredoomed to failure and disappoint-ment but wide open, as well, to misconstruction by those ill-disposed towards you. And of these there will be many.

MISS DACRE turns to address MR DRISCOLL direct. It is an exception to the general rule that no one speaks directly to anyone else.

Miss Dacre: Are you taking it down?

Driscoll: It's all . . . *(taps forehead)* . . . up here.

Mrs Bridgnorth: It's possible nowadays to get a small battery-operated refrigerator . . . purpose-built to accommodate the heels.

Wakefield: One was coming to that.

Mrs Sinclair: After having disposed of the question of the advisability of using a mangrove swamp with its attendant dangers.

Miss Dacre: There is a certain esprit de corps among croc-odiles. Things get round very quickly on the grapevine, and the news that someone is dangling his feet in a provocative way would tend to attract crocodiles like bees round a honeypot.

Mrs Sinclair:	A gastronomic feast such as could not be passed up.
Miss Huxley:	The battery-operated refrigerator purpose-built to accommodate the heels would seem like the answer provided he is warned against the danger of leaving them in there too long.
Driscoll:	A special thawing-out device is on the market which the publicity claims is able in the event of their becoming too cool to put them back into reasonable shape again almost at once.
Wakefield:	I hope these few suggestions are helpful to you. Yours sincerely . . . etcetera.

There is a momentary pause before, as if at a prearranged signal, the six characters get up and without any sense of behaving in anything but the most natural way redistribute themselves amongst the tables. It is done in a very casual and leisurely way, rather like a group of musicians combining themselves differently for a new and different piece.

Miss Huxley:	Far and away the most exciting person I have ever known was changed out of all recognition as a result of having a difference of opinion with a bunch of grapes. Her name was Miss Hopkinson.
Driscoll:	Not *the* Miss Hopkinson?
Miss Huxley:	Isabel Hopkinson.
Wakefield:	Oh, indeed. A woman of great stature. No two ways about it.
Mrs Sinclair:	Incomparably the most important figure to grace the ocean bed in this or any other century.
Miss Huxley:	It was her misfortune — while climbing out of a downstairs window — to trip over a bunch of grapes which had been carelessly left on the windowsill, and in so doing to fall headfirst into a bucket of whitewash.
Driscoll:	There to come face to face, if legend is to be believed, with Saint Francis of Assisi.
Mrs Bridgnorth:	Who was sharing the bucket with a third person who is thought by some to have been none other than the youthful Shelley.

Pause.

Wakefield:	The question has since been asked . . . what would Shelley have been doing in a bucket of whitewash?

Miss Huxley:	Looking for inspiration, one imagines.
Mrs Bridgnorth:	Though what inspiration he hoped to find is not easy to envisage. It seems an unlikely venue.
Driscoll:	Inspiration, moreover, being the very last thing Shelley ever, surely, had to look for. He had far too much already. Scribble, scribble, scribble. He never stopped. He and Wordsworth were two of a pair in that respect, Wordsworth leading by a good few thousand lines.
Wakefield:	Having had a good many more years in which to amass them.
Mrs Sinclair:	Shelley died at the early age of thirty, while Wordsworth lived on till he was eighty.
Mrs Bridgnorth:	So it's unfair to compare them.
Miss Huxley:	It was in the bucket, at all events, that Miss Hopkinson was to see, in a blinding flash, what her destiny was to be. The scales fell from her eyes as with Saint Paul on the road to Damascus as she came face to face with Saint Francis who — after the immediate shock of seeing her arrive so unexpectedly had passed — spoke to her of his hopes and dreams through the agency of the young Shelley, who, with his smattering of Italian, acted as interpreter. Much passed between them of which we have no record, but finally Saint Francis came to the crunch and his words are quoted in *The Life and Witness of Isabel Hopkinson*. 'I', he said, 'have, as depicted by Giotto and other great painters, preached to the birds. I have preached to them until they were glassy-eyed. Whether or not they elect to accept the divine message is from now on up to them. Human agency can do no more. It is no longer to pigeons that we should be addressing ourselves, but to pilchards. They as yet have never been given the opportunity to listen as the Scriptures are expounded to them by someone in whom they could put their trust and to whom they could respond in one voice with a loud Amen.'
Driscoll:	It was all Miss Hopkinson had been waiting for, and without stopping to hear more she climbed out of the bucket, her vocation now clear. The first in a long line of underwater deep-sea missionaries, she was quickly to become a familiar sight on the ocean bed, as she trudged round with Bible and snorkel bringing the word of God to such denizens of the deep as were

	disposed to give her their attention.
Mrs Sinclair:	'Lo, I bring you tidings of great joy!' she said to them, as they swam past, intent upon their own affairs.
Miss Huxley:	Many, to begin with, just looked at her, as though she were some kind of giraffe, perhaps, or a visitor from Mars.
Wakefield:	But gradually one began to notice the odd turbot swimming around in bathing drawers.
Mrs Bridgnorth:	Bathing drawers knitted for it by Miss Hopkinson herself, stung, as she was, into action by the sight of fish of all kinds and both sexes engaging in communal mixed bathing in the nude as though it were the most natural thing in the world, totally without regard to the feelings of the silent majority who were sickened and revolted by the whole thing. It was to these that Miss Hopkinson came as a welcome breath of sanity, reaffirming values they had resigned themselves to having lost for ever, and causing them to rejoice that God does indeed move in a most mysterious way to redress the balance when all seems lost.

Pause.

Driscoll:	Her work, however, was to come, alas, to an untimely end.
Wakefield:	A saga in itself.

Pause.

Miss Huxley:	It was brought to an end by an occupational hazard such as few can ever have been called upon to face.

Pause.

MISS DACRE, who has till now not uttered, rises and with her cup and saucer in her hand moves amongst the others, stirring her tea as she recounts the saga, and stopping occasionally to look out perhaps across the mountains.

Miss Dacre:	One of her watery flock was, as fate would have it, a man-eating shark. A shark with teeth as sharp as a razor. A shark with pretensions,

moreover, to being some kind of Shakespearean fool in cap and bells. Prey to a perverted sense of humour, but meaning no harm, it had taken to going round with Miss Hopkinson and nipping her playfully on the ankle as she went about the Lord's work on the ocean bed. It was an activity that quickly became tiresome, particularly as she was by nature a somewhat short-tempered woman, who reined herself in with admirable self-discipline nevertheless, seeing in this a God-given opportunity to present to her watery flock a living example of Christian charity and forbearance in action. It was to this end that she was careful to take it in good part, making a point of forgiving the shark each and every time it happened.

Wakefield: Until.

Miss Dacre: Until.

Pause.

Miss Dacre: Seventy times seven is the limit to which our Lord enjoined us to go, in the New Testament, in forgiving those who cause offence to us, and this, in arithmetical terms, works out at four hundred and ninety times.

Mrs Bridgnorth: Inevitably.

Miss Dacre: Inevitably there came the four hundred and ninety-first time. Enough was enough, and she lashed out with her Bible. The shark — no great shakes at arithmetic and woefully ignorant of his New Testament — was caught an 'almighty wallop' — to use its own words afterwards — on the dorsal fin. Everything went black, and when it came to itself again, full of remorse, it found it had unintentionally taken a lump out of Miss Hopkinson in the very place where she could least do without it.

Miss Huxley: It was, of course, the end of her work.

Wakefield: The end, too, in a regrettably short space of time, of Miss Hopkinson herself.

Pause. Then, as the short break from conference ends, they gather themselves together to return to the conference room.

Driscoll:	*(getting up first)* Well . . .
Mrs Bridgnorth:	*(follows suit)* Yes.
Wakefield:	All too recognisable a pattern in the affairs of men.
Mrs Sinclair:	Alas.

Finally MISS DACRE and MISS HUXLEY go out together.

Miss Huxley:	The little bit of re-grouping made all the difference.
Miss Dacre:	We took off.
Miss Huxley:	We did.

MR DRISCOLL comes back for his lightweight jacket which he has left hanging from the back of the chair.

Driscoll:	It's often the only way.

All three go off together.

Miss Dacre:	Scrap everything and start again.
Miss Huxley:	Like the French in 1789.
Miss Dacre:	And the Russians.
Driscoll:	*(off)* Not a practice to be indulged in unnecessarily or too often, but one always nevertheless to be kept as it were in the wings for when it really has something to contribute . . . *(his voice has trailed off into the distance)*

Slow fade on empty stage.

Anyone's Gums Can Listen to Reason

Characters

Steve	Twenties
Harriet	Twenties
Frances	Twenties
Mr Brill	Fifties
Mrs Perceval	Fifties
Mr Cantilever	Fifties

*Simple Quaker Meeting Hall. Three or four rows
of wooden benches set like pews across the stage
so that the congregation is facing downstage. Th
congregation consists of STEVE, HARRIET and
FRANCES only, although there is room for
perhaps thirty people. They are spaced out over
the room. They sit silent and natural and
relaxed as the lights go up, their minds open to
whatever the spirit may move one or other of
them to say. For some moments there is silence,
and then, without rising, HARRIET speaks in a
soft, unemphatic voice as though reading a story*

Harriet: There was a sound like small marbles dropping
on to the floor . . . some twenty or thirty of
them . . . and Mr Murgatroyd, clearly troubled
at what he suspected might be the cause,
stepped back from the painting at which he had
been gazing with such intensity until that
moment, and looked down and around him in
consternation. As he turned, I could see that his
lips were drawn in over his gums, as might be
those of someone who had just lost all his teeth.
Mrs Pertwee, who had heard the sound too,

looked at the floor and at once got the message. 'Oh, no!' she cried.

HARRIET falls silent. After a moment, STEVE stands and speaks.

Steve: 'What is it?' shouted Kate from the kitchen.

STEVE sits. After a moment, FRANCES speaks without rising.

Frances: 'It's nothing,' called back Lily, who was also in the room. 'All Mr Murgatroyd's teeth have dropped out, that's all.'

MR BRILL quietly enters and sits by himself.

Harriet: This was indeed what had happened. His gums, for the second time that week, had gone on strike.

Steve: 'It's no good trying to put them back in,' said Mr Murgatroyd, as people began to hand his teeth one by one back to him. 'Not while my gums are in this mood.'

Harriet: 'Surely they can be talked to,' said Father O'Flaherty, who had just come into the room.

Frances: 'Talked to?' said Mr Murgatroyd, with a hollow laugh, 'you must be joking!'

Steve: 'But *anyone's* gums can listen to reason!' expostulated Edith, who until that moment had been lying behind the sofa, fast asleep.

MRS PERCEVAL enters on the next line, and sits, also by herself.

Frances: 'Like hell they can!' said Canon Copley, entering the room, and speaking forthrightly as ever.

Harriet: 'Gums are eminently amenable to reason,' returned Edith, sticking to her guns. 'They're known for it.'

MR CANTILEVER has followed hard on the heels of MRS PERCEVAL and unobtrusively finds a place by himself to sit.

Steve: 'You don't know *my* gums,' said Mr Murgatroyd, ruefully.

| Harriet: | 'This isn't the first time, you see,' said Lily, chipping in. 'It's happened before.' |
| Frances: | 'You should read the Riot Act to them,' said Kate, still fuming. 'All they want is a skive. Put their feet up and have a smoke. Under cover of industrial action. They'd get a piece of my mind if they were my gums!' she said. |

There is a silence for some moments. When the three older people begin to speak, they do so like people striking up a conversation in, say, a bus queue. The only difference is that they speak without actually addressing one another. They are expressing what is in their own minds rather than, as in the case of the younger people, seeming to pick it up out of the atmosphere.

Cantilever:	No hardship for them to stir themselves. Hold a few teeth in position once in a while. It's after all what they're there for.
Mrs Perceval:	They could at least make a show of earning their keep.
Brill:	They've got precious little else to do.
Cantilever:	Mine certainly haven't.
Mrs Perceval:	If they're not doing that, they're kicking their heels and getting bored and making a nuisance of themselves.
Brill:	Or sitting with their feet up.

During what follows, and while the three younger people sit quietly in a state of meditative calm, tuned in to eternity, the three older people gradually start to talk to one another, so that, although they do not change their positions, there is an interplay between them as of people exchanging views in a waiting room and finding themselves in broad agreement.

Mrs Perceval:	There's no gainsaying that a man whose gums are pulling their weight is in a far happier position than one whose teeth are allowed to do as they like because his gums don't care.
Brill:	Firmly anchored teeth are in the main contented teeth.
Cantilever:	Teeth which, come mealtime, will buckle down and get on with the job.
Brill:	With a smile on their lips.

Cantilever:	A smile on their lips and a song in their hearts.
Mrs Perceval:	And not just one tooth at a time.
Brill:	Team spirit.
Mrs Perceval:	All the teeth working harmoniously together — hand in glove — for the good of the whole organism.
Cantilever:	And in partnership with the jaws.
Brill:	In partnership with the jaws to get the food not only chewed but effectively chewed.

Pause.

Cantilever:	Unhappy the man whose upper right molar doesn't know what his lower left canine is doing.
Brill:	A failure in communication.
Cantilever:	Whereby some of the food gets chewed seven or eight times over whilst other food is not chewed at all.
Brill:	And this makes for bad feeling.
Mrs Perceval:	Particularly in the case of food that feels itself neglected but doesn't like to come forward for fear of being thought to be fussing or drawing attention to itself unnecessarily.

Long pause.

Cantilever:	Who was it encountered one of his front teeth at Waterloo Station with a pair of binoculars slung round its shoulders?
Brill:	Haydn.
Cantilever:	'Where are you off to?'
Mrs Perceval:	'Ascot.'
Brill:	They please themselves.
Cantilever:	No amount of remonstrance . . .
Brill:	Oh, no. Couldn't care less.
Mrs Perceval:	I think probably that Galileo had more trouble with his teeth than almost anyone.
Brill:	Particularly his wisdom teeth.
Cantilever:	Which were invariably in the public library whenever he wanted to chew with them.
Brill:	And no change, either, from his incisors.
Mrs Perceval:	His incisors were as likely as not wandering hand-in-hand through some meadow or other picking daisies.
Cantilever:	When they weren't down on the beach watching the tide come in and go out.
Brill:	One might just as well not have any teeth.

Cantilever:	They can lead you a right old dance if you don't watch them.
Mrs Perceval:	Not that I've any complaint against mine, touch wood. They pull their weight reasonably well.
Brill:	Mine, I must say, do a perfectly good job.
Mrs Perceval:	They're not all tarred with the same brush.
Brill:	The last time mine had any sort of break was in 1954. When they went to see Marlon Brando in 'On The Waterfront'. They sat in the two and threes. As it was then.
Mrs Perceval:	Did they enjoy it?
Brill:	They liked bits of it. They weren't, as I remember, any too smitten with the way it was done, but Brando they thought superb.
Cantilever:	Old Mrs Frobisher's teeth were into films quite a lot.
Brill:	Mrs Frobisher's teeth were into everything.
Mrs Perceval:	They led a pretty lively existence.
Cantilever:	Precious little time for Mrs Frobisher in the end, if the truth were told.
Brill:	She had them out eventually. To hell with it.
Mrs Perceval:	You can hardly blame her.
Cantilever:	It's coming to something, when your own teeth not only go to the pictures without so much as a by-your-leave, but choose whereabouts they're going to sit in that lordly manner, and generally carry on as if they were a law unto themselves.
Brill:	I can't imagine anybody in his right mind and with an atom of self-respect allowing himself to be dictated to in matters of that kind by his teeth
Mrs Perceval:	He might consult them.
Brill:	He might consult them, largely out of politeness and to let them feel that they're being kept in the picture, but he wouldn't necessarily feel himself bound.
Cantilever:	A man kow-towing to his own teeth . . . it would be a pretty unedifying spectacle. It's a pusillanimous stance to adopt.
Mrs Perceval:	There's no denying a lot of people do, for better or worse, allow their teeth a fair measure of independence.
Brill:	No one's advocating an unduly authoritarian attitude, but — aesthetic considerations apart and regardless of whether they're qualified or not — to let your teeth make decisions of that nature is to let the tail wag the dog on a pretty gargantuan scale.

Cantilever:	Upper and lower set marching straight to the most expensive seats with their owner trailing ignominiously along behind them is hardly a very uplifting sight.
Brill:	Show me a man who allows himself to be overborne by his teeth, and I'll show you a man who's in deep trouble.
Cantilever:	A sad day for the cinema when that sort of consideration determines what we see on our screens. The cultural life of the country would have to be at a pretty low ebb.

The three older people relapse into silence.

Steve:	All Mr Murgatroyd's teeth were by this time gathered up and handed back.
Harriet:	'What are you going to do with them?' asked Mrs Pertwee, ever practical.
Frances:	'I've got a matchbox,' he said. 'They can go in there.'

Pause.

Harriet:	But, search as he would through all his pockets, no matchbox could be found.
Steve:	It was the work, however, of a moment to drop the teeth into his pocket.
Frances:	Where they remained.

Pause.

Steve:	After a little while, the teeth were beginning to burn a hole in his pocket and he got up and went to the mirror. 'I'm wondering,' he said, 'whether it's safe to put them back in.' 'There's no harm in trying,' said Lily. 'If it weren't for my gums being bolshie, I wouldn't hesitate,' he said.
Frances:	'They want a good belt up the backside,' said Mrs Pertwee, speaking for them all.
Harriet:	'They'll get it one of these days,' said Mr Murgatroyd, slipping his teeth back in one at a time.
Frances:	'Fingers crossed,' said Mrs Grover.
Steve:	'Heaven be praised,' said Mr Murgatroyd, 'they're all back and, so far — touch wood — they're staying put.'

Harriet: 'Oh, yes,' said Kate, appearing at the door,
            'you look a treat with your teeth in.'
Frances: 'He certainly does,' said Canon Copley, and the
            others concurred.
Harriet: 'Now perhaps I can go out and face my public,'
            he said, going out.

            Pause.

Harriet: 'What a fuss,' said Lily, 'about a few teeth!'
Frances: 'Fuss indeed,' said the others, with warmth.

            Pause.
            Slow fade.

Vivienne Welburn

Vivienne Welburn was born in Yorkshire in 1941. After graduating from Leeds University she worked as an English teacher for eight years. She now lives in Chiswick with her husband and two daughters, working as a freelance writer. Her first play *Johnny So Long* was successfully produced at the Traverse Theatre Club in Edinburgh, and subsequently in Australia, South Africa, Israel and at many of the major universities.

Plays
Clearway (Calder & Boyars 1967)
Johnny So Long and The Drag (Calder & Boyars 1967)
The Treadwheel and Coil Without Dreams (Calder & Boyars 1975)

'My principal preoccupation as a dramatist is the exploration of the relationship between inner, subjective reality and external, objective reality and the tension created by that relationship.

Everything which happens in our lives takes place within a social and political structure which is external to us, but the way in which we experience the structure and respond to it is very personal and subjective. These two areas are constantly overlapping and they therefore create ambivalence and confusion. Nothing, for example, is more deeply personal than giving birth to a child and yet population statistics indicate that giving birth is a social act of great concern to the nation and the world. How, then, in writing a play about having a baby, could I clearly indicate both the subjective emotions of the family involved, and the social and political consequences of a population explosion, and the relationship between the two? Or again, how can I portray a relationship between two people on a realistic level and still dramatise the undercurrents of feeling, memory, hopes and fears each carries but is unable to articulate?

I often feel when I tackle this problem that it is a kaleidoscope. The pattern is very clear and organized and then, with a flick, the whole structure changes. The same pieces are there but they have arranged themselves into a different pattern. Each play I write can be seen as an exploration of these different patterns.

The two which I have contributed to this book are very different in style but in the end the basic preoccupation I have described comes through. *Snakes and Ladders* explores some of the rules of group dynamics within a formal, non-naturalistic structure. What kinds of rules do groups set themselves when they meet and what happens if people break the rules — or is it possible to break the rules? Certainly at the end of this play the game has gone too far and moved into reality. Micky is hurt and the external world must be called in to help. Yet each of the group accepts responsibility for the accident, even the victim, as if by some collusion this were a necessary conclusion to the game.

In *Vacant Possession* the convention is much more naturalistic. Two women meet for a business transaction. But a great deal of emotion is invested in houses and Violet's outburst at the end of the play is a culmination of all the tension which has been generated between the two women of different generations and outlook and the emotions surrounding this particular vacant possession.

Sorting out our own values and beliefs from those of our parents and the wider social structure is a job which starts in adolescence and continues on into later years. I hope in working on these plays young people may be challenged to investigate both their outward social behaviour in groups and the nature of their subjective experience as individuals.

Snakes and Ladders

Characters

Topsy

Jane

Sharon

Flora

Micky

Spud

Gus

Wellington

Stepladders and ropes around the stage — the ladders close to the ropes.

The characters file on and stand in a semicircle facing the audience. They stand male next to female and introduce themselves. Their dress is casual.

Topsy:	Hello, I'm Topsy.
Gus:	I'm Gus.
Jane:	How do you do, I'm Jane.
Wellington:	Wellington's the name.
Sharon:	My name's Sharon.
Spud:	Spud.
Flora:	Just call me Flora — like the marge. *(She chuckles.)*
Micky:	I'm called Michael.
All:	*(turning on him)* Micky.
Micky:	All right, Micky.

They all relax and start talking together.

Micky:	*(clapping his hands for attention)* If I may have a word. *(He waves a paper.)* Today it's musical chairs.
Topsy:	That's tomorrow.
Micky:	With respect, it says here *(tapping his paper)* that it's today.
Topsy:	Tomorrow.
Spud:	She's right.
Micky:	Well, if I may say so, it's very bad organization to have agenda papers which aren't correct.
Jane:	I agree.
Spud:	You always bloody do!

Pause.

| All: | Up the ladder, it's snakes and ladders. |

They push SPUD to the nearest ladder and he climbs up. The rest face the audience. WELLINGTON steps forward.

| Wellington: | Yes, folks, today is snakes and ladders day. |

They all sing and dance.

All:	If you win a point It's up the ladder, You lose a point, It's down the snake, It's a game of chance, It depends on the shake Shake, shake, shake.
Topsy:	*(yawns)* It's all a waste of time.
Sharon:	Pessimist.
Spud:	She's alienated.
Gus:	Depressed.
Spud:	*(loftily)* A mindless consumer who's been consumed.
Gus:	And what are you?
Spud:	I'm trying to help.
Gus:	You're manipulating.
Spud:	It's the bloody System.
Gus:	It's bloody you.
Spud:	You're jealous 'cos I'm up here and you're down there.
Gus:	Come down and say that.
Spud:	I'm the king of the castle.

Gus:	Cowardy cowardy custard.
Topsy:	Shut up — you're both *boring*.

Pause.

All:	Up the ladder, up the ladder.

They all turn. TOPSY climbs up another ladder.

Sharon:	Why do you always get up the ladder for being rude?
Wellington:	Aggressive.
Sharon:	Don't caring people get up the ladder?
Gus:	You loved our little fight.
Jane:	*I* didn't.
Gus:	You didn't try to stop it.
Wellington:	He's getting at *you* now.
Sharon:	I think the whole game's wrong.
Spud:	She's got sense.
Sharon:	Who decided the rules?
Micky:	If I may, I'd like to point out that you can't change the rules.
Sharon:	Why not?
Jane:	Oh no, you can't change the rules.
Flora:	Can't do that, love.
Topsy:	We always play this way.
Sharon:	Isn't it time for a change?
Spud:	The new girl wants to be leader.
Sharon:	There *is* no leader.
Wellington:	Oh, yes, there is.
All:	Oh, no, there isn't.
Wellington:	Oh, yes, there is.
Sharon:	*(impatient)* Who?
Spud:	Me.

Pause. They all look at each other and then turn on SPUD.

All:	Down the snake, down the snake.

He scowls then slides down the rope and crawls along the floor like a snake.

Spud:	*(to SHARON)* Sssssss, I'll get you Eve.
Sharon:	*(cool)* The name's Sharon.
Wellington:	She doesn't like you.
Sharon:	I don't like this game.

Micky: If I may I'd like to point out you don't need to be here.
Jane: That's right.
Sharon: *(to JANE)* Why are you so bloody spineless!
Topsy: Don't start on her, she's my friend.
Sharon: She's wet!
Flora: Don't get so worked up, love, just take things as they come, that's what I do.
Micky: With respect, I'd like to say that if you don't understand the rules of this game and don't want to play, you're quite free to leave.
Sharon: I don't want to *leave* — I want to change the rules.
Micky: How?

They all sit in a circle looking at SHARON. A long silence. She looks round helplessly.

Sharon: *(losing confidence)* It seems to me that . . . that it's wrong to win by being nasty.

SPUD blows a raspberry.

All: Up the ladder, up the ladder.

Holding his hands above his head, SPUD goes up another ladder.

Gus: He'll be intolerable now.
Sharon: You told him to go up.
Flora: Don't get so agitated, dear.
Jane: She enjoys it.
Wellington: *(to JANE)* Miaow.
Jane: That's unfair! *(She sulks.)*
Topsy: Welcome back, Spud.
Spud: Lonely were you?

She smiles flirtatiously.

Micky: If I may say at this point —
All: Oh shut up!

Pause.

Topsy: He's no snake to go down.
Gus: He's never risen.
Topsy: He's where he's always been.

Gus:	Stuck at the bottom.
Sharon:	Maybe he's just shy.
Micky:	Thank you.

Pause.

Sharon:	Don't I go up the ladder?

No one speaks.

Wellington:	Anyone got a fag?

GUS throws a pack to him. He lights one.

Wellington:	It's all getting a bit heavy round here. Sharon's trying to stir things up and we resent that as a group, though we may applaud it individually. We are not a happy group today.
Flora:	I'm quite happy.
Gus:	You never take part.
Flora:	Yes, I do!
Gus:	Indignation, well that's a welcome change.
Jane:	I don't like you getting at Flora.
Gus:	But you wouldn't mind me getting at Sharon.
Jane:	*(slight hesitation)* She's all right.
Gus:	You're a liar.
Topsy:	It's lucky you don't know what she thinks about you, Gus.
Gus:	I thought you'd gone to sleep.

He crosses to the ladder and looks up.

Gus:	*(deliberately offensive)* Lovely view.
Topsy:	Glad you like it.
Spud:	*(to GUS)* What're you trying to prove?
Gus:	Eh?
Spud:	Attacking all the women. You won't get up the ladder that way.
Wellington:	He's filling in for you while you're up there.
Spud:	Yes, well I am gorgeous, aren't I?

Everyone groans.

All:	Down the snake, down the snake.

SPUD slides down the snake.

Spud: You appreciate, of course, that I deliberately
arranged for that to happen.
Sharon: Why?

Crossing to stand close to her.

Spud: I had my reasons.

She moves away.

Micky: It seems to me that there are a number of us
just hanging around watching all this happening.
Spud: You don't have to.
Micky: I'm trying to understand the situation and your
arrogance doesn't help.

Pause. The group look at each other and nod.

All: Up the ladder, up the ladder.

*MICKY looks confused and pleased and climbs
the ladder.*

Topsy: I've been here longest.
Wellington: You'll fall eventually.

*SPUD crosses to SHARON again. He touches
her arm.*

Spud: I like you.

She pulls her arm away.

Spud: Don't you want to be liked?
Sharon: Everyone wants to be liked.
Spud: Why are you avoiding me?
Topsy: He's making a pass.
Gus: He's verbally goosing you.
Jane: Aren't you going to do something?
Topsy: Don't you like it?
Sharon: I don't know. I feel embarrassed.
Topsy: *(admiring)* He's just so big. Look at the shoulders
on the man.

*SPUD turns to her and she looks him up and
down.*

Topsy: I rather fancy you myself actually.

She kisses the air at him.

Spud: Piss off.

She looks peeved.

All: Down the snake, down the snake.

TOPSY slides down the snake and brushes down her clothes. She moves over to WELLINGTON.

Spud:	*(to SHARON)* Don't ignore me.
Sharon:	Don't rush me.
Topsy:	He turns you on, doesn't he?
Gus:	What are you ashamed of?
Wellington:	Her sexuality.
Topsy:	Christ, *I'm* not.
Wellington:	That's obvious.
Jane:	Go on, Sharon.
Gus:	Tell him.
Topsy:	Touch him.
Flora:	Touch him.
Topsy:	Feel the strength of him.
Jane:	Smell the smell of him.
Gus:	He's waiting.

SHARON and SPUD face each other. The group stands round them, waiting.

Spud: Just let it happen.

Pause.

Sharon: No. Not now. Not yet.
Spud: No second chances.

SHARON turns and walks quickly to the nearest ladder. She stands there with her back to the audience, very tense.

Sharon: I will not be belittled.
Gus: She's upset.

He crosses and puts an arm round her.

Gus:	He's an arrogant bloody sod, I'm much nicer.
Sharon:	Stop competing with him.
All:	Ah ha!
Micky:	With respect I'd like to point out that someone should have been laddered.
Spud:	Who?
Micky:	If you want my opinion, I believe Sharon deserves to go up.
Wellington:	Now *you're* competing.
Micky:	If you choose to look at it that way, that's your business.
Spud:	I was the one taking risks.
Micky:	In my opinion you lost.
Flora:	Sorry, lovey, you did lose.
Spud:	I made the move. I go up.
Topsy:	My Gawd. He really cares.

SPUD turns quickly to the ladder. SHARON looks across at him.

Micky:	I really must protest, this is nowhere in the rules of this game.
Spud:	Down the snake.
Micky:	No.
Spud:	I said *down*.

He puts a foot on the ladder where MICKY is sitting.

Micky:	*(appealing to the group)* Are we really going to allow him to get away with this?
Jane:	Take a vote. Let's take a vote.
Spud:	Like hell you will.

He shakes the ladder violently. MICKY suddenly loses balance and falls. He screams as he falls to the ground.

Pause.

Sharon:	He's hurt.

She rushes to him.

Sharon:	Give me something to put under his head.

WELLINGTON moves over and takes his jacket off for her. She puts it under his head.

Micky: *(groans quietly)* Where are you? I can't see you.

WELLINGTON examines him.

Wellington: I think he must have banged his head.

The group turn and stare at SPUD.

Spud: Oh God!
Flora: I'll call an ambulance.

The group exchange anxious glances.

Flora: We have to. He needs help.

The group consent, silently. FLORA leaves the stage. Pause.

Wellington: *(quietly to SPUD)* You bloody fool.
Sharon: We let him do it.

MICKY groans slightly. JANE crosses and takes hold of his hand.

Jane: *(to MICKY)* The doctor'll be here soon.
Topsy: I'm scared.

GUS puts an arm round her.

Sharon: *(to SPUD)* You needn't have done it for me.
Spud: Maybe it was for myself.
Sharon: He'll be all right, won't he?
Spud: That's not the point, is it?
Sharon: I'm accepting my responsibility. *(He looks at her.)* I suppose I didn't realise how much you cared.
Spud: That doesn't help Micky.
Wellington: It's beyond the power of any of us to help Micky now. He needs a doctor. I also accept responsibility for this action.
Jane: Include me.
Topsy: And me.
Gus: Me too.

MICKY groans again. They all look ashamed and embarrassed.

Micky: *(faintly)* What about me?

He raises himself slightly, but slumps back. They stand round him with bowed heads.

Vacant Possession

Characters

Violet Watson

Samantha Morgan

A table, two chairs and telephone are at the side of the stage (left), otherwise the stage is bare.

VIOLET WATSON is sitting at the table talking on the telephone. She is in her late fifties, wears bright red lipstick, floral dress and flat shoes; a lively, shrewd woman, left behind by fashion.

Violet: Yes . . . yes . . . yes . . . name? Right *(she writes)* . . . Mrs Morgan 11.30 . . . don't worry dear . . . right you are. *(She laughs.)*

She hangs up and scribbles on a pad. The telephone rings again.

Violet: Hello . . . yes, speaking . . . yes, dear? I see . . . yes . . . yes . . . someone coming any minute . . . could you? Right you are, 1.30 . . . good.

She hangs up.

Violet: *(looking at her watch)* Just time for a quick cup.

She gets up and walks off stage. Pause. The door bell chimes. Pause of a further five seconds and it chimes for a second time. VIOLET appears.

Violet: All right, all right, keep your hair on!

She crosses the stage and exits the other side. Voices off.

Sam:	*(off)* Samantha Morgan, the agent made an appointment?
Violet:	An appointment, yes, come in.

They come on stage. SAM is slim, trendy and in her late twenties.

Sam:	*(looking round carefully)* A bit early, I'm afraid.
Violet:	Not to worry.
Sam:	The last house wasn't worth looking at.
Violet:	Really.
Sam:	Too small. *(Pause)* This is a good sized room.
Violet:	Seventeen six by seventeen six, that's into the bay of course.
Sam:	Yes.

Pause.

Violet: Used to be our sitting room before the children left home.

Pause.

Violet: I had three children.

Pause.

Do you have children?

Pause.

Sam: Yes, two; three and five years old.

Pause.

Violet: Since the children left we've rented it out, students you know, I like young people. Shall we start the guided tour upstairs?

They cross by the table and chairs and climb imaginary stairs. The stage becomes the house with opening and closing of doors mimed.

Violet:	This is bedroom four.
Sam:	Small.
Violet:	Usual rear bedroom. My eldest boy used to have this. Full of model aeroplanes he had it. That

keen on flying I swore he'd grow wings. *(She laughs nervously.)*

Sam: *(smiling artificially)* Really.

Violet: And this is the bathroom — new primrose low-level suite.

Sam: *(not impressed)* Mmmh.

Violet: This is bedroom three.

Sam: Fair size.

Violet: Electric points.

Sam: Rewired?

Violet: Five years ago.

Sam: And the house has been damp-proofed?

Violet: *(nods)* With guarantee.

Pause.

Sam: Fireplace removed I see.

Violet: Lord yes!

Sam: Any original fireplaces?

Violet: In the house — no.

Sam: Pity.

Violet: Great ugly things, had them removed years ago.

Sam: I rather like them.

Violet: Yes, well, tastes differ. Lot of work for women I always say. My husband ripped the lot out.

Sam: Lot of work for men.

Violet laughs.

Violet: Never looked at it like that! *(Pause)* He enjoys working on the house does my old man.

Sam: *(politely)* That's lucky.

Pause.

Violet: Your husband, handy is he?

Sam: *(smiling)* Not that way.

Violet: Did all these fitted cupboards too, mine did.

Pause. They move.

Violet: This is bedroom two.

Sam: Yes.

Violet: Lovely view.

Sam: *(politely)* Lovely.

Violet: Very sunny — floods in.

Pause.

Violet:	We converted this to a kitchen.
Sam:	So I see. *(Pause)* We're looking for a family house.
Violet:	Well this is. We only converted five years ago when the children left. *(Pause)* This is bedroom one, what you call your first floor front.
Sam:	Good size.
Violet:	More fitted cupboards.

Pause.

Sam:	You rented the downstairs rooms?
Violet:	That's right.
Sam:	You still have tenants?
Violet:	*(edgy)* Don't worry, it'll be vacant possession.
Sam:	Good.
Violet:	No worry there, no worry at all.
Sam:	Good.
Violet:	*(changing the subject)* My husband papered all the rooms up here.
Sam:	I see.
Violet:	He's a very careful worker. *(Pause)* It washes down this stuff — miracles of modern science I say.

She chuckles again.

Sam:	Is there a loft?
Violet:	Yes, *(she points)* there.
Sam:	The roof?
Violet:	Very good condition. Shall we go down?

They climb downstairs.

Sam:	This looks like the original staircase.
Violet:	That's right.
Sam:	Very solid.
Violet:	Made things to last in those days, didn't they?
Sam:	Well designed too.
Violet:	This is your dining room.
Sam:	Does someone live here?
Violet:	That's right.
Sam:	She'll be leaving?
Violet:	That's right. She'll be leaving. No problem. This is your breakfast room — french windows to the garden.
Sam:	Very nice.

Violet: A good size. Kitchen there *(acidly)* — original stone sink. More fitted cupboards.

Pause.

Sam: I like the garden.
Violet: All lawn. I'm not much of a gardener myself. I prefer sitting in the sun.
Sam: The children will love it.
Violet: Yes, they do. Little ones need a garden. *(Pause. Softly)* Mine loved it.

Pause.

Violet: My husband built the shed.
Sam: He must work very hard.
Violet: Likes to keep busy. Built the fence too.
Sam: May I see the front room again?
Violet: Of course.

They cross by the table and chairs.

Sam: Original mouldings.
Violet: That's right.

Pause.

We used it a lot when the kiddies were at home but it's too big now.
Sam: I like it.
Violet: There's lots of potential certainly.

Pause. SAM looks round again.

Sam: Yes, I like it very much.
Violet: The house's been well maintained.
Sam: I can see.

She takes out cigarettes and offers one to VIOLET.

Violet: Thanks.

They light up rather awkwardly.

Violet: I was making a cup of tea when you arrived.

Sam: Oh, I'm sorry I interrupted.
Violet: That's all right. Would you like one?
Sam: *(hesitates)* Yes, please.

She sits on the telephone chair, throws back her head and blows out smoke; gazing at the room. VIOLET exits and returns with a tray, two cups, sugar, milk and biscuits.

Violet: Won't take a tick.
Sam: Have you had many people interested?
Violet: Oh, yes. It's a fair price you see, very fair, and the position's good, of course. We had one of those actors you see on the telly commercials. Knew his face but I couldn't place him.

Pause.

          You work do you?
Sam: Yes, I'm a freelance designer.
Violet: Oh, and the kiddies?
Sam: I have a very nice mother's help who comes and takes care of them. *(Pause)* I work at home, of course.
Violet: *(disapproving)* But not with the children.
Sam: *(defensive)* Not all the time. *(Pause)* I need space for a studio. This *(she waves her hands)* is ideal.
Violet: Yes, I can see that.

Pause.

Violet: Is your husband in that line too then?
Sam: No. He works abroad a great deal.
Violet: Navy man?
Sam: No.
Violet: I'll see to the kettle.

Exit. SAM gets up and walks round.

Violet: *(returning with teapot and cosy)* Here we are then.

She puts down the teapot.

Sam: This is most hospitable of you.
Violet: Dying for a cup.

She chuckles.

How do you like it?

Sam: Milk, no sugar, thank you.

VIOLET pours out two cups.

Violet: Sold your own place?
Sam: Yes. We're renting a flat locally.
Violet: So when would you want to move?
Sam: In about two months I suppose. *(Pause)* And you?
Violet: Oh yes, that would suit us.

Pause.

Violet: Are you — local?
Sam: No, London.
Violet: Oh, my eldest boy's in London. A student.
Sam: University?
Violet: Art college.
Sam: Oh, which?
Violet: The Slade. *(Proud)* Very clever at painting, must get it from his father, certainly not from me!

She laughs.

Sam: I'm sure you're right.
Violet: My other boy's in the merchant navy. Doing very well.

Pause.

Sam: And the third?
Violet: Pardon?
Sam: You said you had three children.
Violet: *(evading)* Would you like another cup of tea?
Sam: No thank you.

VIOLET pours herself a cup.

Sam: I'd like my husband to see it.
Violet: Yes.
Sam: Could we come on Saturday?
Violet: Of course, dear.

SAM stands.

Sam: I'm interested. You'll accept an offer?
Violet: I'll consider one.

Pause.

Sam: And you assure me it will be vacant possession.
Violet: *(impatiently)* Yes, yes, I've told you that. She's
leaving. Not staying here any more. Going off
somewhere else. Vacant possession alright.
(Pause) It's been a happy family home. *(Pause)*
Very happy . . . The asking price is reasonable
too . . . very reasonable. . . . We want to move
fairly quickly, you see . . . well you said you did
too . . . It's necessary you see, we need to, it's
necessary . . . so we're asking a very reasonable
price, very reasonable indeed . . . don't you
think? *(Pause)* We were let down badly before,
we really were, they backed out at the last
minute. Backed out . . . no reason given . . .
filth, people like that, really . . . terrible people
. . . terrible. They didn't contact us . . . not a
word . . . stringing us along and then — *(She
gestures with her hands. Pause. More softly)*
That's why it happened *(bitterly)* — *that's* why
— scum, filthy scum, you can't trust anyone, not
anyone, so we weren't really watching her
properly, you see, not really, not the way you
would if everything was normal; all right, you
know? *(Pause)* I always trusted her, of course,
my own daughter, you do, don't you? I mean
you don't expect this sort of mess up, you don't
expect your own daughter — do you? Taken
advantage of she was, that's what it was . . .
*(She puts her head in her hand. SAM gets up and
goes quietly out. VIOLET turns her back to the
seat SAM was sitting in and continues with her
monologue.)*
It's all because of them . . . we could have
stopped it . . . we were just so worried. It's all
because of them. She's a good girl, she wouldn't
have gone and done it otherwise, and then the
accident . . . and so, you see, she'll be going too.
It'll be vacant possession alright, don't you
worry. It's all so unfair. *(Pause.)* They should be
shot people like that —

She turns in anger on the chair.

they should be . . .

She sees the chair is empty and drops her voice.

shot.

Sound of the door slamming off stage as SAM leaves the house. VIOLET sits down exhausted.

Olwen Wymark

Olwen Wymark was born and raised in California. She married the late Patrick Wymark in 1950 and they have four children. Having written some plays for radio, she began writing for the theatre in 1965. Her *Three Plays* won first prize at the Belgrade Festival of New Theatre in 1967. She has since written ten one-act plays, all of which have been performed both in London and the provinces. Her first full-length play *Speak Now* was presented in 1975 at the Haymarket Theatre, Leicester. She has also worked with and written plays for children and for various community theatre groups, and is now Writer in Residence at Kingston Polytechnic.

Plays
Three Plays (Calder & Boyars 1967)
The Gymnasium and Other Plays (Calder & Boyars 1971)

'I intended to be a writer from the age of about twelve. I wrote a great many very heavy and turgid short stories and a lot of extremely embarrassing poetry. Then when I was twenty I married and had four children and there never seemed to be any time for anything but that. In 1956 I began writing radio plays. About six of them were accepted and done but I didn't regard myself seriously as a writer until 1965 when I wrote my first stage play. It was a one-act play called "Lunchtime Concert" and it more or less wrote itself. I didn't have to plan it at all; it just arrived. It was a peculiar sensation and it was rather a peculiar play. It was performed at the Glasgow Citizen's Theatre and was well received and that spurred me on to write more peculiar plays. Quite often I didn't know what they were about until I was halfway through and sometimes I didn't really realise what they'd been about till I saw them on the stage. However, paradoxically, it became more difficult to write them the more I learned about stagecraft.

I have gone on to write for radio and television as well as the stage. I've been very fortunate to have everything I've written performed and I'm still astonished that I can make a living by writing.'

We Three

Characters

Em

Bridie

Girl

*The stage is bare. There is the sound of wind
whistling and crows cawing. EM enters rather
out of breath. She is an old lady dressed in a
long grey dress, small grey hat and grey fur-
piece round her neck. She has a grey blanket
folded over one arm.*

Em: *(calling)* I'm here. I'm sorry I'm late — *(stops)*
Oh. *(Looks round.)* Odd.

*She puts down the blanket and goes first upstage
left and then right peering out, shading her eyes
as if looking into the distance. Then down to
face the audience. She looks out again.*

Em: Nobody. I don't understand this. *(Doubtful)* I
suppose it is the right place. *(Pause.)* Of course
it is.

The sound of the wind and the crows rises.

Em: *(shouts upward)* Oh be quiet!

Immediate silence.

Em: *(irritable)* I should think so. *(She unfolds the
blanket.)* Well there's nothing I can do. I shall
just have to wait. *(She spreads the blanket out
on the floor.)* It's not good enough. *(Stands still
for a moment.)* I shall say something. I shall
certainly speak. *(Resolutely)* Yes. *(Sits on the*

blanket.) There are times when I think I'll give all this up. Just give it up. *(Shouts upward.)* Give it up! *(The sound of the wind and crows rises again and subsides. She sighs.)* Heigh ho.

She gets a stocking and a needle and thread out of her pocket and begins to mend the stocking. She is intent on her work and whistles softly through her teeth.
A figure in a black cloak with feathers sewn on it in bunches and a terrifying mask enters from upstage right. It silently zig-zags down the stage until it is behind the oblivious EM. It raises its arms in a curved threatening gesture and then with terrific speed darts round to the front facing EM and obscuring her from view. It utters a terrible cry and falls in a heap on the floor. EM hasn't looked up and continues mending and whistling for a few moments.

Em: *(putting down her work)* The mask's awfully common.

The figure sits up and takes off the mask. She's another old lady, BRIDIE. She looks at the mask.

Bridie: *(disappointed)* Oh . . . common? Do you think? I thought it was rather exciting.
Em: Well it didn't excite me.
Bridie: You're so conservative, Em. What about the feathers? *(She gets up and twirls round.)* Not bad, eh?
Em: *(sighs)* Always so fancy, Bridie. You wear something different every time.
Bridie: Well it makes a change. I should think you'd get sick of your grey. I get so bored!
Em: *(reproving)* We all get bored, Bridie. *(She resumes her sewing.)*
Bridie: Where's Mollie?
Em: Not here.
Bridie: *(astonished)* What? She must be.
Em: *(tart)* Well she's not.
Bridie: *(moves anxiously about)* But she's always the first. Always. What can it mean?
Em: *(puts her sewing away and gets up)* She's been behaving very strangely lately.

Bridie:	Yes she has. *(Goes over to EM. Confidential)* Last time — did you notice? — she kept leaving bits out.
Em:	Of course I noticed. I lost my place twice.
Bridie:	Did you say anything to her?
Em:	No, but I shall this time.
Bridie:	I wouldn't dare.
Em:	I'm not afraid of her.
Bridie:	*(matter-of-fact)* You are.
Em:	*(ignoring this. Starts to fold her blanket.)* I shall give her a piece of my mind.
Bridie:	If she comes.
Em:	*(stares at her)* She's bound to come.
Bridie:	Yes. *(She walks upstage and then turns.)* Em . . .
Em:	Yes?
Bridie:	Just supposing — I mean I know it won't happen, but just supposing . . .
Em:	*(wary)* Yes?
Bridie:	Well if by any chance she didn't turn up at all — would we have to carry on today anyway?
Em:	How could we? There have to be three.
Bridie:	*(coming down to her. Speaking very confidentially again)* We could just go then, could we?
Em:	*(looking round nervously. Low voice)* I don't know. I suppose so . . . yes.
Bridie:	*(excited whisper)* Em! We could retire!
Em:	Sssssssh! *(then very cautious)* You don't really think we could?
Bridie:	I don't see why not. If the Rule's been broken . . *(Her voice gets bolder.)* Oh Em think of it! What would you do?
Em:	*(dreamy)* I've always fancied a little ferret farm. A few stoats . . . weasles.
Bridie:	Too quiet for me. I'd travel round the fairs telling fortunes. I'd be rich!
Em:	Go commercial? I'm sure that wouldn't be allowed.
Bridie:	Why not? Don't you see, Em? We could do whatever we liked. We'd be free!

There is a high singing cry from off stage.

Bridie:	*(clutching EM)* What's that?
Em:	*(nervous)* I don't know.
Bridie:	*(aghast)* You don't think it's Mollie! What if she heard us?

The cry comes again.

Em: *(feigning courage)* Don't be ridiculous. That's right out of Mollie's range. She's a baritone.

Bridie: *(going over to the side)* There's someone coming!

Em: Quick Bridie, hide! *(Picks up BRIDIE's mask and hands it to her.)* We can't have strangers seeing you dressed like that. Hide!

Bridie: Where?

Em: Here. Get under this.

She unfolds the blanket. BRIDIE gets down on all fours, EM throws the blanket over her and sits on her. A GIRL enters dressed in rags, her face covered in dirt.

Girl: Hello, Missus.

Em: *(prim)* Good afternoon.

Girl: Have you seen my goat?

Em: No I haven't.

Girl: It came this way. Didn't you hear it singing?

Em: *(repressively)* Goats don't sing.

Girl: Mine does. Give us something to eat, Missus. Give us some food.

Em: I haven't got any food. Run along now, there's a good girl.

Girl: Why are you sitting on her?

Em: I beg your pardon?

Girl: Bridie!

BRIDIE stands up suddenly.and EM falls off. They both stare at the GIRL.

Bridie: Who are you?

Girl: *(sits down)* I've come from Mollie's house.

Em: *(gets up)* What do you mean?

Girl: We got there in the middle of the night, the goat and me. We waited all night in the hedge till the sun came up. All red the sun was in the filthy air.

Em: *(mesmerised)* Yes.

Girl: Then the goat sang and I called. *(Calls)* Mollie! Mollie! Not a sound came from the house. Nothing.

Bridie: *(mesmerised)* Nothing.

Girl: There was an ape on the roof of the house. A big grey ape. He stared at us. But then the goat sang again and I laughed and the ape swung down off the roof and ran away. We saw him leaping over the hedges until he was gone.

Em: ⎫
Bridie: ⎭ Yes.

Girl: I went into the house. I searched. When I opened the cupboards swarms of dragon-flies flew out. And bats. Thousands of them humming and squeaking and then out the window like a cloud.

Em: ⎫
Bridie: ⎭ Yes.

Girl: The fireplace was full of dead lizards.

She smiles at them. They stare back. She gets up and walks over to them.

Girl: She's gone. Mollie's gone. She'll never come back now.

Slowly BRIDIE and EM begin to move away in opposite directions.

Em: *(low)* She'll never come back.
Bridie: *(low)* We can go.
Em: *(low)* It's finished.
Bridie: *(low)* We can go.
Em: *(loud. Glad)* We're free!
Bridie: Free!
Girl: Stop!

They stop dead. They try to move but can't.

Girl: Fools.

They stare at her.

Girl: It isn't finished. It's beginning again. You'll do what I say now.
Bridie: I don't believe you!
Girl: No? Dance Bridie!

And BRIDIE begins involuntarily to dance grotesquely round the stage flapping her cloak.

Em: Bridie, don't! Stop!
Bridie: *(still dancing)* I can't! I can't!
Girl: *(laughs)* Yes, you can.

> *And at once BRIDIE falls in a heap on the floor,*
> *panting and sobbing.*

Em: *(furiously)* It isn't beginning again. It can't be.
You're lying!
Girl: Am I? Watch out, Em!

> *EM cries out and clutches at the fur-piece round*
> *her neck pulling at it and moaning. She wrenches*
> *it off and throws it on the floor. The GIRL*
> *stamps on it savagely.*

Girl: *(calmly)* It's dead now.
Em: *(dazed. Holding her neck)* It wasn't alive.
Girl: *(laughs)* It bit you. Get your things on. Quick!
They'll be coming soon.

> *Silently BRIDIE goes and gets her mask and puts*
> *it on. EM picks up her blanket. There is a slit in*
> *the middle of it and she puts it on over her head.*
> *She takes the stocking out of her pocket and*
> *pulls it down over her head.*

Girl: Come.

> *She goes and sits cross-legged centre stage facing*
> *out. BRIDIE and EM go and stand together*
> *behind her.*

Girl: Now!

> *She flings out both her arms. There is a crash of*
> *thunder. Blackout. In the dark:*

Girl: When shall we three meet again, In thunder,
lightning or in rain.
Em: When the hurlyburly's done, When the battle's
lost and won.
Bridie: That will be ere the set of sun.
Girl: Where the place?
Em: Upon the heath.
Bridie: There to meet with
All: Macbeth!

> *Loud crash of thunder.*

And After Nature, Art

Characters

Man I

Man II

Woman

Three people, two men and a woman, sitting round a table. They are looking alertly at each other with extreme amiability and goodwill but nobody says anything. After a moment or so they look away and gaze off into space a little embarrassed. Then one man rubs his hands together energetically, clears his throat and crosses his legs. The other two watch him attentively. He looks back at them earnestly; says nothing. They look away rather awkwardly again. The woman stands up, tugs down the ends of her sweater over her hips. The other two look at her with interested anticipation. She very carefully straightens her skirt over her hips and sits down again. The other two look away as before. Then the second man takes a fountain pen out of his pocket, sniffs it, looks at it, unscrews the top, examines it again. As before, the other two watch this with optimistic attention. He returns the pen to his pocket and again they look away.
There is a pause.
Then the first man sings a note 'La'. The second man, pleased, joins in, his 'La' in harmony. The woman looks anxiously for a moment from one to another as they sing and then with an expression of realisation joins in on a higher note. They hold the chord, not looking at each other, and slowly rise, singing, to a standing position. The chord gets louder and louder. They cut it off abruptly. They smile at each other with great pleasure and sit down, folding their hands on the table.

Man I:	*(brisk)* Well, I expect the first thing we should do is to decide which of us is Arthur.
Man II:	*(vigorously)* Absolutely!
Woman:	*(enthusiastic)* Yes, yes!
Man I:	*(looking at her uncertainly)* I don't really think *you* can be Arthur. It *is* a man's name . . .
Woman:	*(hurt)* Oh I think that's awfully unfair.
Man II:	Unfair? It's bloody outrageous! My God, haven't you ever heard of Equal Rights?
Man I:	Oh sorry . . . of course . . . silly of me. *(To WOMAN)* I beg your pardon.
Woman:	*(kindly)* Not at all.
Man I:	I don't know what got into me.
Woman:	Please. Don't give it another thought.
Man II:	*(rather excitedly)* I say . . .
Woman:	*(sharply)* Be quiet, Arthur. Don't interrupt. Your father and I are having a conversation.
Man II:	*(disconcerted)* Wait a minute. I don't . . .
Man I:	Arthur! Do as your mother tells you!
Man II:	*(sullen)* It isn't fair.
Woman:	*(resigned smile to MAN I)* Oh dear, dear, dear.
Man I:	Come on, lad. Get if off your chest. What isn't fair? You can tell us. We're all pals, aren't we? Chums?
Woman:	*(very expansive)* One big happy family!
Man I:	*(reproving)* One big *un*happy family.
Woman:	*(shuts her eyes)* I forgot. *(She puts her hand over her eyes.)*
Man I:	*(shocked. To MAN II)* You've made your mother cry!
Man II:	Well gosh, I only . . . I mean Charlie's mother and father let *him* interrupt. Edward's mother and father let *him* interrupt. *Every*body at school interrupts *their* mother and father all the time!
Woman:	*(looking up. Shrewdly)* Have you brushed your teeth? Those fingernails are filthy.
Man I:	When I was your age I wasn't allowed to have a toothbrush. We were too poor. Or a colour telly.
Woman:	Or piano lessons.
Man II:	I've lost my piano.
Woman:	*(irritable)* Oh Arthur! When did you have it last?
Man I:	How many times do we have to tell you you must take care of your things. We can't always be keeping an eye on your piano, you know. Your mother and I are busy people.
Woman:	I said you could have a piano but I did say you'd

have to feed it yourself, didn't I? I've got too
much to do washing your P.E. kit without
looking after a piano.

Man II: *(querulous)* You're always getting at me.

Woman: *(amazed) Getting* at you?

Man I: What a way to talk! What a thing to say!

Man II: See? I can't say anything! It really depresses me.

Woman: *(laughs indulgently)* Depresses you! You're far
too young to be depressed.

Man I: It's only a phase. You're a very normal, happy,
well-adjusted boy.

Woman: You *love* rice pudding.

Man I: *And* you love going to visit your Uncle Bert and
Auntie Mabel.

Man II: I hate going there!

Woman: Oh yes, you have such fun playing in the garden
or reading old copies of the National Geographic
while the grownups talk.

Man I: And you're very happy at school.

Man II: *(increasing desperation)* I'm not!

Woman: You want to be a bank manager when you grow
up. Just like your daddy.

Man II: I don't!

Woman: You don't smoke.

Man II: I do!

Man I: You're not a bit interested in all this loud rock
music.

Man II: I am!

Woman: You really enjoy keeping your room tidy and
doing what you're told. You've never given us a
moment's trouble.

Man I: Of course not. We understand you.

Man II: You don't! You don't even know me! I'm
leaving. I'm running away from home and I'm
never coming back!

*And he gets under the table. There is a pause.
The other two look at each other alarmed and
immediately stand up and walk about behind
the table looking anxiously round, their eyes
shaded by their hands. They are both absolutely
serious.*

Man I: *(low, urgent)* There's no one here.

Woman: *(angrily nervous)* How do you know? You can't
possibly be sure of that.

Man I: Trust me, Arthur.

Woman:	*(wringing her hands)* I can trust no one! No one!
Man I:	You're safe here, I promise you. I'll protect you. Would I have followed you here if I didn't care for you? Who else having seen you singing wild songs in that telephone box, having seen you running down the dark street in the deserted village your mouth open in a soundless scream — who else would have dared to follow you?
Woman:	You shouldn't have followed me. You did wrong to come here. *(Passionately)* Can you not see that this is the last place of all? *(Scornful)* Protect me? Protect me from the eagles that will come soaring and cutting the sky and screaming my name? Protect me from the terrible wind which will blast through that forest till all the trees roar and howl *my name?* You! Protect me from the monstrous, misshapen beast that lurks in those caves? Crouched . . . waiting. Waiting to call my —
Man II:	*(from under table in deep voice)* Arthur!
Woman:	*(terrified)* Oh God!
Man I:	*(clutching her arm)* Don't answer it, Arthur. Don't answer.
Woman:	*(clapping her hands over her ears)* I'm afraid!
Man I:	Quickly! Quickly! We'll run away. *(He pulls at her arm but can't move her. He tries to run himself but is rooted to the ground)* I can't move!
Man II:	Come, Arthur, come. I have waited a long time.
Woman:	*(takes a step toward table as though pulled)* I know.
Man II:	There is no way but this, Arthur.
Woman:	I've always known. *(Another step forward.)* There was never any hope. Only this.
Man II:	Only this. Waiting for you. Waiting to devour you — to swallow you up. Come, Arthur. In the belly of your nightmare you will be safe. Never to hear your name again. Come!

And with a cry the WOMAN falls and goes under the table. MAN I, with a desperate gesture, covers his face with both his hands, his head up. He holds this in silence for a moment, then takes his hands up and away from his face holding them together as if they were an open book. Looks efficiently at the palms of his hands.

Man I: Thirty third street . . . *(looks at imaginary sign post)* Yes, yes. Thirty third street. And . . . *(looks at palms again)* Theta Avenue . . . *(looks at another sign)* Yes. *(Closes his hands together and mimes putting the book into his pocket.)* Now. Number nine. *(Moves along looking out toward the audience.)* Number seven . . . number eight . . . Ah! *(Stops. Facing table)* Nine!

He knocks briskly on the table.

Man II: *(comes out. Smiles)* Good morning.

Man I: Good morning. I've come about the advertisement.

Man II: *(cordial)* Ah. You must be Arthur.

Man I: That's right.

They shake hands.

Man II: *(suddenly stern)* You're late.

Man I: *(nervous)* Oh I don't think so. It said exactly . . .

Man II: *(interrupting)* Just a moment. *(Leans down and speaks to the WOMAN under the table.)* He's here.

Woman: *(coming out)* Ah. Arthur is it?

Man I: Yes it is . . . I mean, I am.

Woman: You're late.

Man I: No honestly . . . I checked my watch by the pips on Radio Three. I'm sure I'm right and the advertisement did say –

Woman: Sit here please.

She puts one of the chairs on the table facing upstage. She and the MAN II watch MAN I clamber up and sit down. Then the two of them sit facing out on either end of the table so that MAN I has to crane round to look at them.

Man II: What is the complaint?

Man I: Er . . . *(He looks from one to the other, puzzled.)*

Woman: We need to know your complaint.

Man I: But I haven't got one. I just came along because . . . Oh. Now. Do you mean complaint as in illness?

Man II: *(bit bored)* If that's what it is. Are you ill?

Man I: No. No I'm not.

MAN II and the WOMAN look at each other and sigh.

Woman:	*(sharp)* What stand do you take on the Irish problem?
Man I:	Well it's not an easy question to answer . . .
Man II:	*(interrupts)* Have you taken any concrete steps toward solving the population explosion?
Man I:	Do you mean me personally? Er . . . I'm not *married*.
Woman:	And the plight of prisoners in labour camps? Have you taken any action on that?
Man I:	I? How could I? I mean of course I *disapprove* of it but —
Man II:	The whole question of pollution — how much progress have you made there?
Man I:	*(agitated)* Well not a lot . . . I mean it's not my *fault*, is it?
Woman:	*(surprised)* Certainly it is.
Man II:	Of course.
Woman:	What about the shortage of staff in mental hospitals?
Man II:	Slum clearance?
Woman:	Battered babies?
Man II:	Famine?
Man I:	*(to one after the other)* Wait! Wait!
Woman:	*(angry)* Wait for what? When are you going to start doing something?
Man II:	What have you done so far?
Man I:	Nothing — but after all I'm only —
Woman:	*(horrified)* Nothing?
Man II:	*(unbelieving)* Nothing at all?
Man I:	*(desperate)* What *could* I do?
Woman:	Do you call yourself a human being?
Man I:	Well yes I . . .
Man II:	Don't you care about anybody but yourself?
Man I:	Yes I do. Of course I do but . . .
Man II:	*But* — you've done nothing.
Voice off:	Arthur!
Man II:	Oh sorry. Must dash. *(He goes off in direction of voice.)*
Man I:	Where's he gone?
Woman:	*(surprised)* They called him.
Man I:	But it's me. I'm . . .
Woman:	Yes it's you we're discussing. You and your appalling failure to do anything at all for any of the misery that —

Voice off: *(from another direction)* Arthur!
Woman: Oh that's me. Excuse me. *(She goes off.)*

> *MAN I looks off in the direction she went and then in the direction of MAN II's exit.*

Man I: *(to himself)* But it isn't her . . . *(He stands up and gets off the table and lifts the chair down.)* Or him . . . *(He sits on the chair looking depressed.)* I don't understand. I mean it's not *them* at all. It's . . .
Voice off: Arthur!
Man I: *(with great relief)* Coming! *(and he goes.)*